MW01148280

PRAISE FOR

WARREN RUSTAND

Warren Rustand is one of the finest people I know. He also possesses something that has become quite rare in this world: WISDOM. Listen to what he says, apply it—with intent!—to your life, and good things will come your way. It's as simple as that.

—**Matthew Reilly, International Best-Selling Author**

When Warren speaks, we all listen. And we should. I'm delighted to see his inspiring stories and clear pathways to leadership success outlined in this fabulous new book. I have personally been encouraged and awed by Warren's dedication to always bringing his best energy to the time that he has. He has blessed thousands of leaders across the globe in his live presentations, and I know this book will continue to expand his kindness and wisdom for many generations to come.

—**Heidi Hanna, *New York Times* Best-Selling Author**

More than anyone I have ever met, Warren Rustand has helped countless others to clarify what they want most, to live and lead according to their values, and to elevate expectations both for themselves and those they lead. His impact on an entire generation of future leaders is immeasurable, and I am excited to see him share his wisdom in a book for the first time.

—**Bob Glazer, CEO of Acceleration Partners and Best-Selling Author of *Elevate* and *Friday Forward***

I have known Warren Rustand for more than twenty years in my roles as the CEO of two international not-for-profit associations. During that time, he has been an inspirational and aspirational leader, espousing these leadership principles and positively impacting the lives of literally thousands of global business leaders through events, writings, and personal interactions. I have incorporated these principles to help me become a better business leader, a better husband and father, and a better person. This is a thoughtful, masterful study of leadership and its relevance, and is a "must read" for anyone wanting to truly achieve a "life by design."

—**Bob Strade, Former CEO of the World Presidents' Organization and former CEO of the Entrepreneurs' Organization**

When I face a difficult challenge, I often write "WWWD" at the top of a page in my journal—"What Would Warren Do?"

I have known Warren for over a decade and worked closely with him for the last five years. Before I met Warren, I believed that to be a successful business leader you had to make sacrifices in your family and personal life. Warren taught me to get clear about who and what is important. Warren's influence helps me focus on what is important. Warren encouraged me to stop comparing myself to others and to focus on becoming a better version of myself. In my talks and lectures, I quote Warren on a daily basis. I love Warren because not only does he know this leadership stuff, he really lives this stuff.

—**Conor Neill, Professor of Leadership at IESE Business School, President, Spain of Vistage**

Warren Rustand is the most humble, generous, and selfless leader I know. With all that he has accomplished and experienced in life, he could have chosen, like so many others have done before him, to pursue the highest levels of celebrity and fame in any area he desired. Instead, he chose a unique path of leadership through serving others so that they may benefit from his experiences and be empowered to achieve their life goals, identify and live by their values, and uplift others to do the same. Warren is generous in sharing his knowledge of how he achieved a successful life based on simple and practical methods with those who want to achieve the same. The impact of Warren's "principles of leadership" on me has been profound, both personally and professionally.

—Rana A. Batterjee, AuD, Author and Entrepreneur

Warren Rustand is in a league of his own and sets the high-water mark in every facet of his life. As a family man, person, entrepreneur, or mentor—his leadership principles and teachings in each of these areas are guiding lights for us to follow to achieve our goals and live a purposeful life. These principles are not theoretical or academic but rather practical teachings drawn from his own life experiences, learnings, and practices. Coupled with his masterful storytelling and anchored by his humility and compassion, they give Warren the superpower of positively impacting people's lives across cultures and nationalities. They have certainly transformed my life.

—Mazen Omair, Founder and CEO, Momair Trading LLC

Exposure to Warren's foundational principles of leadership has sparked dormant values systems alive in my being; they were always there but needed a name, a reminder, a grounding. Warren's teachings have been consciously authored from a life of servant leadership and then condensed down and organized into a practical toolset for everyday use. As an entrepreneur, a wife, and a mom of five, I have seen Warren's teachings transform my effectiveness and intentionality in each moment. There are not enough thank-yous. I am so grateful.

—MacKenzie Richter, Mother of five

Warren has a tremendous ability to help people tap into and ignite their sense of purpose, which ultimately leads to living a life fully expressed, with great meaning and incredible impact. Time and time again I've witnessed the power of his words and stories to ignite great things in people ... to eliminate excuses and obstacles, get clear on what matters, and then take relentless action. Warren inspires everyone to want to be the best possible version of themselves!

**—Jenny Evans, Author, Speaker, and
Human Performance Expert**

Both subtle and accessible, this book offers keys to creating more successful outcomes in each of our personal, family, business, and community lives. Written without pretention and guided by a strong moral compass and clear vision for the future, The Leader within Us *helps answer questions we may all be asking ourselves. Warren Rustand has guided me and many others to challenge conventional thinking on how to move through the world, sharing simple and sensible ideas for the incremental shifts that have proved rewarding.* The Leader within Us *includes practical, everyday resources for all of us to design our lives and go live them.*

—**Alison Diboll, CEO, Gabriella Rossetti**

WARREN RUSTAND

FOREWORD BY ROBERT M. GATES

THE LEADER WITHIN US

Mindset, Principles, and Tools for a **LIFE BY DESIGN**

ForbesBooks

Copyright © 2020 by Warren Rustand .

All rights reserved. No part of this book may be used or reproduced in any manner whatsoever without prior written consent of the author, except as provided by the United States of America copyright law.

Published by ForbesBooks, Charleston, South Carolina.
Member of Advantage Media Group.

ForbesBooks is a registered trademark, and the ForbesBooks colophon is a trademark of Forbes Media, LLC.

Printed in the United States of America.

10 9 8 7 6 5 4 3 2 1

ISBN: 978-1-95086-325-9
LCCN: 2020916525

Cover design by Megan Elger.
Layout design by Wesley Strickland.

This custom publication is intended to provide accurate information and the opinions of the author in regard to the subject matter covered. It is sold with the understanding that the publisher, Advantage|ForbesBooks, is not engaged in rendering legal, financial, or professional services of any kind. If legal advice or other expert assistance is required, the reader is advised to seek the services of a competent professional.

Advantage Media Group is proud to be a part of the Tree Neutral® program. Tree Neutral offsets the number of trees consumed in the production and printing of this book by taking proactive steps such as planting trees in direct proportion to the number of trees used to print books. To learn more about Tree Neutral, please visit **www.treeneutral.com**.

Since 1917, Forbes has remained steadfast in its mission to serve as the defining voice of entrepreneurial capitalism. ForbesBooks, launched in 2016 through a partnership with Advantage Media Group, furthers that aim by helping business and thought leaders bring their stories, passion, and knowledge to the forefront in custom books. Opinions expressed by ForbesBooks authors are their own. To be considered for publication, please visit **www.forbesbooks.com**.

I dedicate this book to our large, loving family,
of which I am just one part.

The most important part of our family is my wife, Carson. She has been a tower of strength, love, patience, forgiveness, and faith. She has been a marvelous example of a life well lived according to her design and is unwavering in her commitment to her beliefs and principles, which guide her decisions. She has been an excellent role model for me throughout our shared life as I have grown and learned to be a husband, father, and grandfather. I am very fortunate and grateful to have built this beautiful life with her.

Our children have been the beauty and the wonder of our marriage. All seven have brought joy, happiness, fun, and adventure into our lives. Due in part to our farm living, we share a unique closeness and spend a great deal of time with each other. And in doing so, I have witnessed their lives as they have evolved. I so admire each of our children and what they have become through their own intelligence, passions, values, efforts, capacities, and abilities. Each has found success on their own and within their families, while remaining very close to their siblings. They show me every day how to live a better, more intentional life. We have been blessed with our children and acknowledge their positive influence in our lives.

Our grandchildren are the rising generation. I have so much hope for them. They represent the very best of our collective futures and the viability of our planet. They are bright, fun, adventurous, loving, sensitive, and kind. They are so present, conscious, informed, curious, and aware. They have wonderful parents who have taught them well and love them so much. I believe each of them will honor their family, serve their community, live their purpose, and make choices that will influence others and issues for good. I love all nineteen of them with all my heart.

Our family stands at the very center of all I do. It is the essence of who I am and is at the core of my very purpose. Without them I would not be the man I am, nor could I have completed this book. I am humbled by and forever grateful to them. May they always feel my love.

CONTENTS

FOREWORD

By Robert M. Gates

I first began working with Warren Rustand more than forty-five years ago. Warren was President Ford's appointments secretary, and I was on the White House National Security Council staff working for Henry Kissinger and Brent Scowcroft. We became friends as we traveled around the world doing the advance work for the president's travel. It was often stressful and routinely exhausting as we hopped from one world capital to another, often trying to sleep as the plane sped through the night. I quickly realized that Warren was a very special person—always positive, upbeat, good-humored, and exceptionally competent. His devotion to his young family was readily apparent. From the earliest days, I was impressed with his integrity, self-discipline, ability to prioritize, and focus on the long-term objective. These multiple positive attributes have been a constant in Warren's life through the ensuing decades as he has led one organization after another.

Now, in this slim volume, Warren has distilled the lessons of life and leadership that have contributed to his success as a husband and father, businessman, philanthropist, and community leader. Most books about leadership focus solely on a person's professional life.

This one is unique in applying the concepts for success at work also to success at home—and to personal fulfillment. Warren believes, as do I, that there can be no difference in values between the personal and professional. Integrity is indivisible.

Warren properly devotes a considerable part of this book to the personal traits a leader must have for success at home and at work. He brings his points to life through the stories of specific individuals he has encountered and mentored through the years, stories that are at once compelling and moving. In each the reader experiences firsthand what Warren refers to as the "Five Principles of Personal Greatness." His lessons range from the general—self-discipline—to the specific—managing your time better.

Leadership is more than just managing well. A leader is defined as "a guide, one who shows the way." A leader must have both a vision of what an organization can become and the ability to devise strategies and tactics to achieve that vision. This volume is a how-to manual to accomplish both based on Warren's own experiences and those of others. He describes the importance of being always ready to learn new things, to embrace new ideas. The world is never static; the only constant is change. A real leader must be an organization's agent of change. Warren helps the reader think about how to do that—how to develop a blueprint for making significant changes, for setting and achieving goals. Baseball legend Yogi Berra once said, "If you don't know where you are going, you will wind up somewhere else." This book offers guidance on how to identify the right destination and how to get there.

Warren offers a great deal of practical advice in *The Leader within Us*. One important theme is how a leader must avoid being overwhelmed by the constant distractions of the day—whether emails or people wanting to pop into the office for a brief chat—and must make time to think. As a senior executive at CIA, president of Texas A&M University, and secretary of defense, I only half-jokingly would look at my daily calendar and observe that it was a plot by the bureaucracy to keep me so tied up in meetings that I had no time to meddle in what they were doing. The more time I spent working on their agenda, the less time I had to work on mine. As Warren points out, the only way to alter that dynamic is to set aside (and guard ferociously) time during the day to shut the door and think—to work on one's vision, strategy, and long-term objectives. *The Leader within Us* is full of such pearls of wisdom.

Warren devotes considerable space in the book to the importance of family and life-work balance. Washington, DC, is full of people who like to brag about their eighteen-hour days, seven days a week, and that it has been years since they took a vacation. I was always suspicious of such folk and often concluded it was either because they were hopelessly inept at doing their work or were so insecure they were afraid that if they took time off, their absence might not be noticed, thus imperiling their job. As secretary of defense, I led the largest organization on the planet—three million military and civilian employees and a budget of $750 billion a year. I routinely left the office by six or six-thirty in the evening. I always took a briefcase of work home, but I wanted to give all those who worked for me a chance to get home and have dinner with their families and time with their children. I knew if I stuck around the office, hundreds of people would do likewise just in case I called. In over four-and-a-half years as secretary under two presidents, I never once went into the office on a weekend. Again, I wanted those who worked for me to get rested and to have time with their families. And every summer I took two-week vacations. During World War II, General George C. Marshall, with twelve million men under his command and at war, left the office midafternoon nearly every day and went horseback riding. He was wont to say that no good decision was ever made after 3:00 p.m. Warren Rustand's *The Leader within Us* brilliantly addresses the importance that healthy body, healthy mind, happy family have for successful leadership.

It is a rare thing to be able to pack so much wisdom into so few pages, but Warren has accomplished that feat. The principled man of strong personal values and full of the joy of living whom I met in 1974 has not changed. Over the decades, though, he has accumulated extraordinary experience and insight into the leadership of organizations and people. *The Leader within Us* is his legacy. And it is a most valuable one.

INTRODUCTION

A Momentous Day at the White House

It is not often that you find yourself standing in the middle of history.

But on August 6, 1974, at the age of thirty-one, that's exactly where I found myself. America was in turmoil. Protesters were in the streets. The Saturday Night Massacre had gone down. Articles of impeachment were being drafted for the president. The Supreme Court had ruled on the secret Oval Office tapes, and everyone was talking about the Watergate scandal.

As the recipient of a prestigious White House Fellowship, I was at that time working in the office of the vice president, Gerald Ford. As such, amid all the uproar, all the confusion, and the disorder, I heard the words that had been spoken by a senior White House official: "Mr. Vice President, prepare to be President."

Like I said, it's not often that you find yourself standing right in the middle of history, and here I was, right there in it.

And do you know what I remember most about that day? Watching Vice President Ford take in this news, absorb the enormity of it, and then move into action. He saw, with clarity, what had to be done and knew that only he could do it. He said to contact specific people and have them attend a transition team meeting the next morning. It was one of the finest moments of pure leadership I have ever seen.

With startling speed and poise—while under pressure—Ford saw exactly what he had to do, determined how he would do it, and then directed the steps by which it had to be done. I have had a lifelong interest in leadership—one that has extended into the five decades since those wild times—and I dare say that you will be hard-pressed to find a better example of it than this. On August 9, 1974, I led the vice president into the East Room of the White House for his swearing in as he became the president of the United States.

But I am getting ahead of myself. I will tell you a little later about how I came to be in the White House and what other things I both accomplished and learned along the way.

For my intellectual journey into the principles of leadership didn't begin at the White House. It began well before that, when I was a boy living on a farm in Minnesota with limited indoor plumbing.

It began with me observing my father.

Lessons on a John Deere

It was seventy years ago, but I remember it, all the details. I was six and driving the John Deere for the first time on our farm in Minnesota. The big John Deere, not the little one—the tractor that was supposed to transform me from little helper to real-life farmer. It was the tractor that my dad could point to with pride and say, "Warren can handle it; he's a natural."

But I wasn't a natural. I was a failure. I was backing the tractor down a slight incline to attach the plow, which had come unhitched, when it hit a large rock. I couldn't stop the tractor while backing it up, and I soon became pinned down by the levers of the plow against the steering wheel. I couldn't breathe. I couldn't reach the gearshift. I couldn't move at all.

I remember blood trickling down my back; I struggled to take one more breath and realized I couldn't. But then I felt big, strong hands around me. The tractor began to move, and I could breathe again. My father had come for me just in time. He had been working hundreds of yards away, but he had been watching over me, and he had come to my rescue.

While he certainly saved my life that day, there have been countless times since where I could look back and see, without a doubt, that my father has come to my rescue through the example he set for me and the knowledge he freely and joyfully shared.

A Father's Example

We had limited indoor electricity and no indoor plumbing on the farm, and, as you might imagine, Minnesota weather in the wintertime was a little difficult. My dad was well educated and had a corporate job in the Twin Cities prior to being asked to return to the farm and operate it for his eleven brothers and sisters, following the deaths of his mother and father. Over time he acquired the shares of his siblings and owned the farm outright. My dad loved the farm, and so I loved the farm.

My father, Stanford, was the hardest-working man I've ever met. He was always industrious, and he had a bias toward action. There are many talkers in life but fewer doers. My father was a doer and I think by his example helped me live a life of doing.

My father was also the first to tell me there was more. Much more than the small-town Minnesota farm life I loved. As I sat on his lap, he would drive the tractor, plowing the ground or gathering crops, singing, talking about people and about events he had attended and why they impacted him so deeply. He talked about education and farming and family.

When we were doing work around the property, he talked about books he'd read and what he learned. He often quoted a poem to me that I remember. The poem is called *Think*.

I think I'd rather not think, for thinking is like a disease.

I know I'd rather not know, for stupidity comes with such ease.

And not so much stupid as content with the state,

going through the day knowing only that I ate,

but to think means to live and to live means to do,

and doing is what is done, but only by a few.

The experiences he shared painted the world in my mind as if it were boundless and that anything was possible in it. Even though I was young—four, five, six years old—he felt it was important to share these conversations.

I didn't realize until more than a decade later that what he was doing was preparing me for a life that was different than the one he himself was leading. He was actually engaging me, intellectually, as a young boy to think about life differently. Because I thought about life differently, I thought everything was possible. Therefore, I had more options than just living on that farm.

When we went to town or when people visited the farm, I noticed he talked with people openly and easily. Everywhere we went he would create conversations with people, even if he didn't know them initially. He was very social, whereas I was more quiet and shy at that time. One day I asked him why he talked to everyone. He said something very important to me: "Everyone has a voice and a story, and we should listen to that voice and their story."

If my childhood sounds idyllic, I guess it was, but it was also just what you might expect Minnesota farm life in the 1940s to be. Hard work, long days, and often freezing. Although limited in her education, my mother worked very hard alongside my dad to make sure the farm ran well.

Like any good brother, I tried to kill each of my sisters at least once, but my first pony, Dinah, must have been on their side, because she'd bite at me anytime I tried to saddle her. My horses now are a bit friendlier. So are my outstanding, intelligent sisters. They've had great careers and have done well, all predicated on intelligence and hard work.

Moving to California

When I was eleven years old and in the fifth grade, my dad decided we should move to Southern California, and I started to see some of that boundless world he'd told me about. I was introduced to a variety of sports and new cultures, ethnicities, and religions. Someone introduced me to basketball during junior high school. I enjoyed it and began playing.

I was still a little quiet and shy as I started high school but became less so as I made friends and developed more of a social life. I also determined that I wanted to break out from being quieter to developing my father's skills, which were very social. I thought the best way to do that was to get involved in sports, so I ran cross country and played baseball and basketball.

I had worked hard and accrued some honors and awards, but I had also amassed a bit of an ego. My outlook was overly simple and finite; I only saw that every opportunity was rising up to meet me. I didn't yet have the humility or experience to understand that opportunity would not simply be given; it would have to be chased and earned. I would have to intentionally pursue those opportunities—be willing to work and wait—for them to come to fruition. And I was about to learn a great lesson.

At about the midpoint of my junior year of high school, the wrestling coach, Clint South, who was a mentor, teacher, and a man I admired, had a conversation with me. During this time I was flexing my ego and, I imagine, offending others. Mr. South sat me down one day and said, "You know, you're a real jerk, and your ego is beyond bounds. Unless you change, you will not have any friends." That was a stunning wake-up call coming from a man I admired and liked. And as a result of that, I made some fundamental changes. It was a great lesson, and I always admired his willingness to step forward and be transparent, vulnerable, and authentic with me about something I needed to hear.

Once I got my ego under better control, I thought it would be good for me to get involved in student government because I was interested in leadership; even at a very young age, I was intrigued by people who led. I ran for junior class president, won, and discovered that we had a phenomenal class of scholars, athletes, thespians, and musicians. At the end of that year, I determined that I would run for student body president, which I did, and won.

We had almost a thousand people in our graduating class at California High School in Whittier, California. And I recognized that we had an opportunity to set a special standard with this class. Even to this day, over fifty years later, our class of 1961 at California High School is regarded as the best class that's ever graduated in terms of athletics, scholarship, theater, and musical talent. Many went on to have distinguished careers.

What I found in applying my dad's strategy that everyone has a voice and a story that needs to be heard was that when students were able to find common ground, they could more easily work together toward a common goal. That enabled us to build consensus, to collaborate, and to engage with others in ways that enhanced decision-making and created better processes. The result was that we had an exceptional year and were able to encourage several thousand students to excel.

By the conclusion of that year, I had won honors and awards for basketball from the California Interscholastic Federation, served as body president, and won the Merrill P. Freeman Award, which goes to the outstanding graduate based on leadership and character.

As I look back on those years, I can see moments that changed me and great moments of clarity and decision-making that shaped my life. I didn't always have the philosophy I have today, but elements of that philosophy were being put in place and developed. I could see that clarity of vision, certainty of intent, and the power of values were all present and being molded. These three principles were refined over the next decade as I clarified the important drivers in my life.

The University of Arizona

I attended the University of Arizona on a basketball scholarship. I chose the U of A over many other schools because of a basketball coach—a man I just knew would have a positive impact on my future. His name was Bruce Larson, and he had been the National Basketball Coach of the Year at Weber State University. He had great basketball IQ, but more importantly he was an exceptional man with strong personal values. I was a part of his first recruiting class at Arizona. He had recruited six talented scholarship players from all over the country, who would become part of the greatest freshman basketball team in University of Arizona history.

My teammates were not only talented basketball players but

also remarkable individuals from whom I learned a great deal over my years with them. One teammate, Bill Nicholson, was also my dorm roommate—a farm kid from Great Bend, Kansas. He made our journey together fun and interesting, from his style of dress to keeping a bottle of vodka in the room's air-conditioning unit. He has been a good friend for all these many years. When I went to the White House, I invited Bill to be my deputy, and ultimately he became my successor when I returned to Arizona.

How have I described Warren Rustand over the many decades we have been friends? As a Human Centrifuge! He has a global galaxy of diverse friendships for starters; then add his art of listening with a wonderful capacity to recall, and that is a great baseline. Then he spins it all together and voila—he gives you the simplest common denominator for your specific situation. Truly unique.

—Bill Nicholson, Entrepreneur and Investor

As I entered the University of Arizona in 1961, it was an interesting time in American history. It was the middle of the civil rights movement and the early stages of the Vietnam War. This was a time when four of our national leaders were assassinated: Malcolm X, John Kennedy, Martin Luther King Jr., and Bobby Kennedy. These events and other social issues were critically important and helped shape me as I pursued my university degree. While there was some controversy on campus, campus life was a lot of fun, and there were many opportunities for social, athletic, and leadership growth and development.

It was during these first few weeks at the U of A that I met three people, each of whom would have a very important impact on my life and the ways in which I would process information and people. Each of them was very helpful in assisting me in developing perspective.

The first, and most important, was a young coed by the name of Carson. She was intelligent, kind, fun, and beautiful. I was introduced to her by a mutual friend, and I immediately asked her out. She said no. I asked her out the next week, and she said no. Again the third week and again no. I asked her out for fifty-three consecutive weeks, and each week it was no.

Now, I am persistent and determined, so I asked her out the fifty-fourth week knowing that the man she was dating was out of town and I had a chance. She again said no. I started acting silly; soon she was laughing, and out of pity, I'm sure, said she would have dinner with me. By 10:30 p.m. that night, we had determined it was probably unnecessary for us to date others. We were married two years later and have been married for fifty-six years.

The Value of Great Friends

There were two men among many whom I met at the University of Arizona who had a big impact on my life. The first was Gayle Hopkins. Gayle was raised in Oklahoma, in a mostly black community. I'd been raised in Minnesota and Southern California in virtually all-white communities. As I came to Arizona, I really saw for the first time a diversity in language, culture, religion, ethnicity that I hadn't seen previously in my life.

Gayle was a track star at the university when I was playing basketball, so we met as athletes and developed a great friendship. Gayle was an outstanding man, and he shared his life journey with me. His story as a young black man gave me a greater understanding of the struggle, difficulties, and challenges in our society to which I had not previously been exposed. We spent hours talking about our respective backgrounds, families, and feelings. He helped me understand, in a very personal way, what the civil rights movement was all about at the human level.

Many years later, when I was advising the athletic director at the U of A, Dave Strack, he indicated that he wanted to diversify his staff and asked if I knew anyone I could recommend. I told him the person he should hire was Gayle Hopkins, who was then athletic director at San Francisco Community College. This was after he had won an Olympic silver medal in the long jump and had earned his PhD.

I called Gayle, and he was interested. After a single interview, Gayle became the associate athletic director at the U of A and was there for some thirty-five years prior to his death. He did an outstanding job, and he continuously contributed great insight to the university and its athletes and all those with whom he had contact.

In the same vein, I met another African American man, Olden Lee, who was a football player at Arizona. He was an air force veteran, slightly older than the rest of us, and he brought a maturity to everything and every discussion. He and I became good friends during our time at the U of A.

I admired him for how he carried himself, how he thought, the way he embraced people. He was an excellent football player. But more importantly he was an exceptional man who helped my understanding and perspective on matters of humanity, social justice, equity, fairness, and decency. He served as a role model for me in many ways.

Olden raised a wonderful family and, always the leader, went on to become the global leader for human resources for all of PepsiCo, and through that background and insight, he has helped me find exceptional executives for positions with companies that we have ended up owning or leading. He has contributed significantly to his communities and the University of Arizona Eller College of Business.

Olden and I have been friends for nearly sixty years. We still see each other regularly, and I still learn from him. I think having friends and close relationships with people of high quality has helped me immeasurably. I encourage you to seek out friends with whom you can develop this same kind of relationship, who will always hold you to a higher standard and expect the same from you.

I appreciate the influence of both of these exceptional men and the friendship they have shown me.

I have known Warren over half a century and have been able to personally witness many of his experiences and accomplishments. His resume reveals the exposures and learnings that make him eminently qualified to expound on the essential qualities of leadership. His ability to both articulate and model the behavior makes him an ideal champion of the topic.

—**Olden Lee, Former PepsiCo Human Resources Executive**

Setting My Sights

Early on I wanted to continue to participate in student government as a learning process. I was asked to participate in the redesign of the student government structure at the University of Arizona, which included student representation in a newly designed student senate. I served as the first parliamentarian of that senate, which gave me great insight into the leaders on campus and what student government could be. A year and a half later, I was elected student body president and had a clear vision of what I wanted to accomplish.

In the area of social issues, and specifically civil rights, I thought it was appropriate that we create a speaker series at the U of A where we would bring people to address the campus community. Some would turn out to be controversial, some not.

The very first speaker we invited was James Meredith, the first African American integrated into the University of Mississippi. We followed that a couple of weeks later with Governor George Wallace, who was a segregationist governor from Alabama. We were trying to bring contrast to different points of view, and we continued that intentionality throughout the speaker series. The ASUA Speakers Series is still alive today and serving the greater community of Tucson.

In addition to that, we wanted to give students the opportunity to be involved in service and understand the notion of servant leadership, engaging in a cause greater than oneself. We decided to create a camp for underprivileged children, run by students, so we established Camp Wildcat and had our first group of attendees during my senior year. This created an opportunity for students to serve young children. Camp Wildcat continues today. (An unfortunate aside—a close friend, Jim Muir, had the idea for Camp Wildcat. About sixty days after graduation, he was killed by a land mine in Vietnam.)

The university was a very important point in my life and a significant part for development purposes. These experiences served as a preamble to the balance of my life.

While at the U of A, I learned a great deal through my engagement with others. I also began to see how my decisions don't just affect me; they also affect those around me. I direct my path, and I am solely accountable and responsible for my decisions. That's why I asked my future wife out every week for an entire year before she finally said yes. That's why I joined the army voluntarily instead of waiting to be drafted during Vietnam. That's why I continue to seek clarity of vision and certainty of intent in the design of our lives today.

After college I was drafted by the San Francisco, now Golden

State, Warriors. I played only briefly and, ultimately, decided I wanted to play with the most successful AAU team in the country, the Phillips 66ers.

We had a great season and ended it by playing for the AAU National Championship. Following the season I was chosen to play for the USA Basketball Team in the World Basketball Championships in Santiago, Chile. We won the silver medal. It was a wonderful feeling representing the United States and sharing that with other outstanding basketball players from all over the United States.

I never forgot the early lessons of my father and the influence of my coaches, friends, and family, all of whom helped me in my definition of vision, intentionality, and values. I was certainly imperfect in this process, but I continued to learn, grow, and apply that which I was learning. Those lessons helped me when I started my career, leading my first company when I was twenty-four years old. Those same lessons carried me to the White House and beyond, as I built, bought, and sold companies; as I started a family; and even now, as I continue to mentor entrepreneurs all over the world.

Global Educational Organizations

Over forty years ago, I joined an international group of CEOs called the Young Presidents Organization (YPO). When a member becomes fifty years old, they graduate into the World Presidents Organization (WPO). YPO/WPO has members in some 150 countries. They organize learning events for members all over the world for the expressed purpose of continuing education for leaders.

For some thirty years, I chaired a public policy conference in Washington, DC, for YPO/WPO titled "Public Policy and the Private Sector." Each year we would host approximately two hundred members of YPO/WPO to meet with the president, vice president, cabinet secretaries, the leadership of Congress, members of the Supreme Court, leading journalists and lobbyists to assist them in better understanding how public policy is made and how they might access the process. In the period I chaired this conference, we hosted over six thousand CEOs. In 2000 I served as the global chair of WPO.

About twenty-five years ago, I began mentoring companies and CEOs in another global organization called EO (Entrepreneurs Organization), which is comprised of fourteen thousand entrepreneurial leaders of fast-growing companies. Its purpose is to be the "most influential community of entrepreneurs in the world."

Thirteen years ago Dave Galbenski, who at the time was the global chair of EO, had an idea to create a global leadership academy for EO, and I was invited to participate in the initial meeting. We created the structure and process for the Global Leadership Academy, which meets annually in Washington, DC. I was asked to be the dean of learning, and I continue in that role today. This brings together the best and brightest entrepreneurs from all over the world for the purpose of learning more about leadership in all aspects of their lives.

There has been a long list of outstanding EO leaders with whom I have worked to make the Global Leadership Academy an exceptional learning experience. Among them: Erick Slabaugh, Carlo Santoro, and Michael Caito. For the past four years, I have co-led this with George Gan. George is from Kuala Lumpur, Malaysia, and is a very successful businessman, an outstanding entrepreneur, a thought innovator, excellent leader, and has a wonderful family. He's also a great friend and EO leader. And he introduced me to the term *Shoshin*.

I had the opportunity to work closely with Warren at the EO Leadership Academy, where he taught and shared his principles and applications of leadership. This book is a must for any entrepreneur or leader seeking to transform their lives and live to their best potential. These tools are simple and effective and will change your life and set you on the path of living a life by design. Thank you, Warren, for your friendship and gift of leadership.

—George Gan, Founder, Silicon & Sand

Shoshin: "The Beginning Learner"

Shoshin is a Buddhist concept that means the beginning learner, being open to new things, to be open-minded.

The Shoshin learner is always in a state of readiness, always trying to learn new things, always trying to improve. As we become more and more expert in things, we oftentimes become more and more narrow, less willing to embrace new ideas. We develop the feeling that we know more or know enough about a particular subject. But we can always keep growing and learning, as the following story illustrates.

There was a husband and wife who purchased a new home, and they had a bank of windows, part of which looked into the backyard of their neighbor. Oftentimes on sunny days the neighbor would come out to hang clothes on the line to be dried by the sun. The couple would come down for their morning coffee, and they would look into the backyard. The wife would say to the husband, "It's so sad that no one has taught her how to wash clothes." The clothes were always dirty. This happened on multiple occasions as they would come down to have their morning coffee and breakfast.

On one particular morning, they came down to have their

coffee, and the wife looked into the backyard, and seeing the other woman hang the clothes, she exclaimed to her husband, "Look, honey, someone taught her how to wash clothes. The clothes are all clean." And the husband said to the wife, "Not really, sweetheart. I came down early and washed the windows."

When we change the way we look at things, the things we look at change. So, as you read this book, I'm asking you to take out the lens through which you see the world, clean it off, put it back in, and be open to new ideas. Put the filters through which you see and hear the world in a state of suspended animation to allow yourself to be open to new and, perhaps, different concepts.

This may be the only moment in time when you and I share this space and time. Let's be in a state of Shoshin, open to new ideas, thoughts, and opportunities.

Life by Design in Arizona

The summers here in Tucson are hot and long. This place we have chosen with our family could not be more different than Minnesota, with its harsh winters. There is a reason we are here. There is a reason I still keep horses and drive a John Deere tractor and sit outside at dusk to look at the acres of land around me. There is a reason I often have a grandchild or two on my lap as I mow or haul rocks on that big green tractor. Because I chose this.

I still love being a gentleman farmer on our land in Arizona. When I'm out on my tractor, sometimes I think about my father, Stanford, and I'm grateful for the time he spent with me. Without a doubt the biggest lesson my father taught me was that the power of work, the power of example, and the power of influence all pay off when you consistently make an effort.

I saw, as a young boy through my father's eyes, and again in the Pacific Ocean, and again at the University of Arizona, and the White House, and the basketball court, and the boardroom—that intentionality and choice are what make us.

I'm writing this book for two reasons. The first is to explain what I believe are the most important principles of leadership and living, and to help you, if you choose, to implement these principles I use every day. The other is to tell you about my life, because my journey is the real story. I can't explain one without the other. My experiences in life helped me create this methodology, and this methodology has helped me build my life as I've chosen to live it.

This life we have chosen to live came through thousands of small choices and scores of big ones. We have learned things along the way that I'd like you to consider. We have chosen to live this life, to be surrounded by family, people, and work we love.

We worked for this, every day, so that our lives would be one of our design. We created the architecture and vision for our life by design. You, too, can create your best life if you are willing to embrace the principles that will follow in this book. You merely have to apply these principles daily for the outcomes you desire.

CHAPTER 1

CHOICE AND DISCIPLINE LEAD TO GREATNESS

It always seems impossible until it's done.

—Nelson Mandela

In 1926 a man flew a single-engine airplane from Long Island, New York, across the Atlantic Ocean, and landed in Paris, France, nearly thirty-four hours later. As this was the first solo nonstop trans-atlantic flight, and being that the pilot was barely twenty-five years old, he made quite the spectacle. But his success was not without great preparation. If Charles Lindbergh had awakened one morning and decided to fly across the ocean in a borrowed plane on a fluke, he may never have been heard from again. Instead, he had a dream, set a goal to achieve it, and worked toward it steadily with a team of people who were able to visualize his success before it ever happened. Lindbergh later wrote about his record-breaking flight, and the dream that started it all, in *The Spirit of St. Louis*: "Now we live, today, in our dreams of yesterday; and, living in those dreams, we dream again ... "

Following his sound logic, it's not difficult to see that the dreams we had yesterday, fueled by choice and action, are responsible for exactly where we are today. And the dreams we conjure up today are exactly what we're going to live in tomorrow. We have to be very thoughtful about what we're dreaming and what we're thinking about because our dreams are creating our reality.

This isn't one more book about simply dreaming something you want into existence. The world doesn't need one more book about manifesting new results and a new life without putting much effort into the exercise at all. Instead, this book is a blueprint for making significant changes, setting and achieving your goals, and living a life you can be proud of ... and doing it the only way I've ever known—with good old-fashioned hard work and determination.

I don't believe in sugarcoating the message to make the delivery any sweeter. I believe that if you want to change some part of your life, you are absolutely capable of doing so. In fact, I believe you're capable of doing more and achieving more than you've probably thought possible. I also know you're equally capable of getting in your own way time and time again.

So, if you're not exactly where you want to be, if you're not yet living *in the dream*, accept it. Own your life. Don't put it off on anybody else and stop making excuses. Accept the responsibility for where you are, who you are, and what you are. This is your baseline, your foundation on which to build.

We cannot change the past, but we can create the future. Let's focus on being the great leader, the great spouse, the great parent, the great athlete, the great human being we really want to be. Let's be that person starting today.

We need to understand that it's a process to get from where we are right now to where we will one day be. There are foundational principles that, once you begin to implement them, will aid you in making the journey from point A to point B simple—*not easy*, but simple.

Along with anecdotes from my life and career—from growing up on a farm, to my unlikely path to the White House, to leading and creating multiple businesses—I'll share stories of people who've transformed their lives, their futures, and their families by doing the work and by not backing down, even in the face of heartbreaking challenges. If you want to change your life, I'll give you the formula. But you have to put in 100 percent of the work.

Thought (Inner) versus Skills (Outer) Leadership

I believe there is an inner journey and an outer journey to our lives. The inner journey is how we think, the decisions we make, what we believe—our core values. I estimate that the majority of our life is inner journey. The balance is the outer journey.

There are certain skills we need to move through the world. We need to know how to break a five-dollar bill. We need to know how to speak in public. We need to know how to manage time. We can teach those skills, and I do teach those skills to many CEOs. This is the outer journey.

The inner journey is a way of thinking about our lives directionally and philosophically. It is a mindset. As Gandhi said, "What I say is what I believe, and what I believe is how I act."

Types of Mindset

In her book *The New Psychology of Success*, Carol Dweck distinguishes between the fixed and growth mindsets. The fixed mindset embraces the current reality as the right reality. The mindset of this person is to make the most out of the current state. Change is inherently a threat to that current reality. The status quo should be maintained.

In David Zelman's book *If I Can, You Can*, he explains that the growth mindset sees situations and circumstances as unique opportunities for learning. Every event tells us how we can learn and improve. The growth mindset is predicated on the idea that one's basic qualities can be developed through effort. Self-acceptance is accepting oneself as an extraordinary, limitless human being.

The basis for Dweck's and Zelman's thoughts is the type of conversations we have with ourselves. Are they automatic and fixed or intentional and growth-oriented? Dweck is focused on the characteristics or results of one's internal conversations rather than the conversations themselves. She suggests that the mindset allows for certain actions and orientations based on whether one has a fixed mindset or a growth mindset.

Other contemporary terms for mindset are *scarcity and abundance* or *infinite and finite*. Each have their own definitions, and I encourage you to review them all. Why is mindset important, and why do I invite some thought and clarification on this subject? Throughout this book I am focused on the positive, growth, abundance, and infinite mindset. This mindset is the essence of our ability to change, transition, and transform. I believe altering one's life is more difficult to do with a fixed, scarcity, or finite mindset. Our understanding of these fundamental definitions is important to our consideration of the principles presented here. Given this, I believe Dweck and Zelman capture my thinking the best on what the options for our mindset can be.

It is up to you to make a choice regarding your preference. The question is this: Would you rather be guided by and engage in a life with a fixed mindset or a growth mindset?

Liberation lies in the ability to choose between an intentional and automatic conversation with yourself. The key is that you have the right to choose. Now exercise your rights.

Starting with the End in Mind

Stephen Covey was right when he said we should start with the end in mind. Determine what outcomes we seek and then work backward from there. This will give us the clearest view of our effort to achieve our vision.

My hope is that this book creates pivot points and decision points in your life to make transition happen. In the aggregate people learn how to transform their lives by applying very specific principles. I want people to be in the transformational process. As you read real stories from real people who have used these principles, you will see that no matter where you begin, no matter your age or ability or circumstances, there is always the possibility for growth, for redemption, and for success.

Now that we've covered the goals, let me step on your toes just a bit.

I believe most of us are average. Most of us want to live a life of comfort and predictability, not of risk and exceptionalism. Those who are comfortable with the status quo, who are comfortable being reactive and not proactive, make up the majority of people in the world. They thrive on routine, continuity, consistency, repetitive effort, and on simply going through the day, doing what they normally do from sunup to sundown, and then doing it all over again tomorrow.

Think that sounds harsh? Many of us talk about working out. Many of us want to lose ten pounds, or stop smoking, or run a marathon. But there is a smaller percentage of people who are going to *decide* to do that, and discipline themselves to achieve that. When they do that, they change their lives forever. They now know that physically, emotionally, and psychologically they can be different because they've done something more.

But there are a great many more of us who may never know that feeling and that level of success. Why? Because we can't bring ourselves to change our daily routines. We might think about how great it would be to go to the gym and start training for that 10K we've always wanted to run. Or we might feel a few moments of excitement when we think about what it would look like to finally write up that business plan for our own company. But we still aren't willing to change our routines, to actually go to the gym or write up that plan. We get stuck in the comfort of predictability and repetition.

How many chances do we really get? How many days do we really have left to make that difference? To run that race. To build that company. To save our marriages and our families. To keep ourselves from one day lamenting, "I wish I'd done more with my life."

Our current lives are the compilation of every choice we've made. Our futures are still unwritten and are dependent on the choices we make next. The great news is, we always have the power to *change*. And we always have the power to *choose*.

> People don't hand us greatness. We decide to be great and then discipline ourselves to be great.

In *Good to Great*, Jim Collins said, "Greatness is not a function of circumstance. Greatness, it turns out, is largely a matter of conscious choice, and discipline."[1] This book is written for those of us who can

---

1   Jim Collins, *Good to Great: Why Some Companies Make the Leap ... and Others Don't* (New York: HarperCollins, 2001).

understand that very premise—we must choose greatness. People don't hand us greatness. We decide to be great and then discipline ourselves to be great. It's about choice and discipline.

The Twenty Percenters

The age-old eighty-twenty rule, which applies to many things, suggests to us that perhaps 80 percent of people are content with their lives as they are; the other 20 percent are itching for something else. For different circumstances and better outcomes. They want to do more and be more. They want to excel. Those are the people who want to change their habits, rituals, and patterns. It's just that they don't know how to do it. And they fear that if they get started, they'll become easily sidetracked, lose momentum, and feel as though they failed.

Guess what? Life is one lesson after another, and we can't fully appreciate our successes if we haven't experienced failures. Yes, we are going to fail, and more than a few times. I've failed many times. But I've also succeeded more times than I've failed because I didn't give up. If I can, you can.

Instead of letting our thoughts dictate our worth after we've missed the mark, use each stumble as a learning opportunity, and try something different next time. That's all we have to do to keep forward momentum. If we follow a particular set of routines, and do it consistently, we will fundamentally alter our lives.

When I present this material to people who've never heard it before, I'm usually met with universal enthusiasm and acceptance because people inherently know that they could and should be doing more. I challenge every audience, no matter the makeup or how successful they seem to be. Time and time again, I say, "We're not doing enough. We're not living our possibilities."

I regularly speak at MIT to groups of EOers, all of whom are very successful entrepreneurs and business leaders. I start by telling them, "You've only scratched the surface. You're not anywhere close to your full potential. You're not doing anywhere near what you're capable of doing, and why aren't you? It's because you don't know how. I want you to consider a formula for doing this. By the end of today, you'll have an understanding of the formula, and you can begin implementing it tomorrow. This isn't something for which you have to wait. You don't have to have a spiritual awakening or a life-changing experience to make you do this. This is something you can simply do, starting tomorrow morning."

The results have been remarkable. People have improved their lives, their companies, their marriages, and their families. It becomes a different world for them. And they aren't the only ones who have seen incredible growth, so don't think you have to already be a C-level executive, a professional athlete, or a member of Mensa to change your life in dramatic ways.

I have worked with an incredible cross section of people. Some have come from success, some from failure, and some have had their fair share of both. Some of them started as I did—humbly. Others began with much more. The common thread is the notion that they are meant to achieve more, do more, push further. Regardless of circumstances, all of these people seem to have a strong commitment to purpose and discipline. They have decided that they can design the life they live.

The people who know me best understand that I simply choose to live my life by design, and, therefore, I may get different results. Once we live our lives with vision and intent, we will begin to see our desired outcomes.

Three Principles of Leadership ε
Five Principles of Personal Great

This content is shared in two parts. Part One consists
Principles of Leadership." These have been learned, ⸺ ...d
practiced over six decades. These three principles are the philosophical
and directional framework and architecture needed to move forward.
These three important principles are:

Clarity of vision

Certainty of intent

Power of values

Part Two consists of the "Five Principles of Personal Greatness,"
and these are focused on the application of the three principles stated
above. These five principles of application are:

Commit to a higher level of personal discipline

Live with purpose

Act with intent

Make conscious choices

Engage in a cause greater than yourself

These principles require action and a consistent effort. There is
a pattern of success, and when principles are applied in a particular
way, it increases and enhances the chance of success.

I've learned these eight leadership lessons, personally, across
the broad spectrum of athletics, community, politics, business, and
family. I've built a good life on these principles but more importantly
thousands of people have now applied these principles and have had
remarkable success.

ι ve heard hundreds of stories of leaders, spouses, parents, and dreamers who have lost it all, fought back, and found even greater success than before. That is the resilience of overcoming adversity. These principles bring greater discipline, which develops greater resilience, which helps to overcome adversity.

One more point: I mentioned earlier that you didn't need to be a CEO to utilize these principles. And that's absolutely correct. These principles directly relate to success in *all areas of life*. I would offer that the quickest way to achieve success in family, business, community, and self is to first exhibit control over your own life, your own time, and your own priorities.

> These principles directly relate to success in all areas of life. I would offer that the quickest way to achieve success in family, business, community, and self is to first exhibit control over your own life, your own time, and your own priorities.

Greatness Is Created

Greatness is a choice. Not necessarily greatness as the world would value it, but greatness for ourselves. If each of us takes a step toward our personal greatness, then our lives, our families, our workplace, our community, and our world get a little bit better.

Wherever we are in our lives, we can determine a way to be great at those things that we choose to do. We can be great at being a father or mother, great at our job, great at helping others, great at our education, great at being kind, great at being a neighbor, and great at being a friend. Greatness is something of which we are capable.

Greatness means not taking the path of least resistance. Not taking the easy road, the road most traveled. Not doing what everyone else is doing. Not being average in anything. Not following the herd, going with the crowd, or following the trends. Not saying and doing what everyone else seems to be saying and doing.

It also means that you will make a determination to do what you believe to be important and true for yourself. It is a point of departure and a willingness to follow your path, even if it means going alone. It is a critical choice and a pivot point for you in your life.

Many look back on their lives and wish their lives had turned out differently, that they'd made other choices. While we can't do anything about our past, we can certainly decide our future. We can apply principles and practices that have worked for centuries so that our life begins to approach the best life we can have, and we can become the best version of ourselves.

Each of us, regardless of our station in life, can decide to do things better, differently, harder, more intelligently, and with greater purpose. This is not complex; it is quite simple.

So, let's start with the first three value-based considerations from which we can create a context for building our new commitments based on simple principles.

The Value of Time

In the history of mankind, our individual lives are but a nanosecond in time. We are an important but short part of history. It was just a short moment ago we were children playing, then teens, exploring, then we were young marrieds, having children and grandchildren, and then in our more senior years. It all goes so fast. We were young and invincible, and now many of us are mature and in some ways vulnerable. Our world, which used to move so slowly, now moves at an exponentially faster pace, seemingly an ever-increasing pace.

In this process of living, we are given 86,400 seconds a day to live. It expires each midnight, and we hope we get another 86,400 seconds. If we live to be seventy-five years old, that is seven hundred thousand hours or twenty-eight thousand days.

If you do the math right now for yourself, where are you in your life? If you are forty years old, you have already lived half your life. Is your life all that you wanted it to be at the halfway point? Is everything in your life precisely as you planned it? Have you accomplished everything you wanted to do? If not, then perhaps reading a little further will illuminate your thinking about the next half of your life.

It's true there is nothing we can do about our history, but there is a lot we can do about our future. We can determine, now with more experience, what we want our future life to be. We can create the architecture and design for how we want to live our life moving forward. We can build the framework and the structure, just as we would build a house. Successful people do just that.

Great lives are forged by grit, determination, and strength. Even though we will build the future, we can be sure there will be adversity, surprises, serendipity, disappointments, even failure. But we also know there will be wonderful success as well. It is the nature of our human condition and journey. Not all is predictable, but we can control our reaction to all things that occur to us as we travel life's roads.

Let's be sure and value the time we have. Don't take tomorrow for granted or assume it is yours. Rather, let's construct our lives using every available moment. Let's be committed and conscious with our time. Let us be present and in the moment. Let us give back what we have been given.

The Value of Life Experiences

One of the great gifts we receive is life experiences. We learn so much from them that we should spend more time thinking about lessons learned from our experiences, both good and bad.

Like you, I have had both in my lifetime. I admit to making silly, stupid, naïve, and even idiotic mistakes and judgments during my life. I have, like you, also been given great opportunities and blessings that I probably didn't always deserve. But, nevertheless, our life experiences are our greatest teacher.

When I worked at the White House with President Ford, we had a tennis group that played when we had the time. And, as you might imagine, we were ferociously competitive.

During one match Dean Burch, chairman of the Republican National Party, and President Ford were on one side of the court, and I was on the other side with George H. W. Bush, director of the CIA. Dean Burch hit a short lob; I drifted back for the lob and hit it with all my power. Unfortunately, it went off my racket at kind of a strange angle. And—*boom*—I hit the president of the United States right in the diaphragm. He went down like a bull moose shot with a gun.

We rushed over to his side and I was thinking to myself, I've killed the president of the United States. With a tennis ball! My second thought was, I am unemployed.

At first there appeared to be no vital signs. He was just lying still on the court surrounded by the Secret Service. Pretty soon he started coughing, spitting, and wheezing. We helped him up. Finally, he put his arm around a Secret Service agent, pointed to me and said, "Kill him."

I said, "Mr. President, some decisions can only be made once!" That's a life-ending decision. Thankfully he wasn't serious. And I learned a valuable lesson that day—don't hit the president with a tennis ball.

Have we taken the time to really analyze that which we can learn, or should have learned, from those uniquely personal things that have happened to us? Have we really framed those essential questions we need to ask ourselves about our decision-making, judgments, and frame of mind, after we have had either good or bad times?

Perhaps the greatest education we have are those memorable times through which we pass. They are unique to us, unlike those that happen to anyone else. No one else has our DNA, fingerprints, genetic makeup, or physical body. Out of 7.5 billion people, we are not like anyone else on planet earth. Therefore, our life experiences are unique to us.

How then can we value them as a learning platform for just us? How do we view ourselves in this light? How can we learn the lessons that are designed just for us, the ones from which to learn?

We should always be the student, always looking for the lesson, always having an open mind. We should ensure that our emotion and passion do not inhibit our learning opportunities. Life experiences are rich for personal development, perhaps even better than a formal education. Can we see clearly the chances for personal learning and growth?

The Value of Life's Challenges

There are certain times in all of our lives when we are very directly challenged by the circumstances of life. The time that we hoped would never come. The stark reality of our own mortality or something so grave that it stimulates the very core of who we are. Those things that happen that we are secretly hoping will never come to our doorstep.

Each of us has such events in our lives, some of our own making, some at the hands of others, and some made by God. When these happen it quickens our breath, floods us with emotion, creates murkiness of thought, and often overwhelms us. It is at these times we discover who we are at our core. We are challenged in a very real way.

Sometimes it is macro in nature—an economic recession or depression, for instance. It is chaotic for our jobs, security, feeling of comfort, or our sense of well-being. There are very real consequences to the issues we face. It can affect our entire family, extended family, and neighbors. It is beyond our control, and there is often a sense of isolation or lack of an ability to influence the event.

The events that shape the world many times have impact on our very own lives. Something that happens a world away comes back to change our very lives, as seen with COVID-19. This pandemic is having significant health consequences in all countries in the world. The sickness and deaths are tragic to be sure. It is so hard to realize, as I write this, that nearly eight million people have been infected and over 200,000 have died, just in the United States, and the end is not in sight. The financial and economic losses are also devastating. Millions of people infected, hundreds of thousands dead, and millions more who have lost jobs, businesses, and economic stability throughout the world. For many the results of the pandemic will take years, decades, or perhaps several generations to recover from. Due to the rapidity of reporting of the actions of governments and people around the world, it seems as if we are getting information in real time. Decisions being made in disparate locations throughout the globe can have reverberations in our own communities.

This is true today as we witness demonstrations in most of the major cities of the world over issues of race, social justice, and economic dislocation and disparity. These are fundamental issues, which must be addressed by governments and citizens in most countries of the world.

These essential inequities have to be reconciled with all stakeholders participating in the solutions and policies that move us forward. I am hopeful we can discover our clarity of vision, so that we can act with certainty of intent.

We truly live in global societies, and what happens in one part of the world can affect every other part of that world. As opposed to overreacting, we must create context and understanding as to motivations and possibilities so that we can comprehend what is occurring and find the path forward for all of us.

And finally there's a notion that there seem to be more tragedies, on a larger scale, that are occurring than we have previously felt or seen. Hurricanes, tornados, earthquakes, flooding, pandemics, and fires—catastrophic events seem to be ever present. Perhaps the reason is that we have more rapid communication systems than ever before.

Social media reports firsthand accounts and gives us a direct connection to on the ground activity. It gives us a front-row seat, a vivid picture of the trials and tribulations of other people, as we witness some of the most difficult events in history, all of which can leave us feeling somber and sad. These circumstances allow for a global empathy for those affected. Yet all of these, in the aggregate, can be hard for us to absorb.

Crises, whether local, regional, or global, get our attention. As we focus on them, it can take us down one of two roads. One is the spiral of feeling bad for others and thinking of the negative aspects of the tragedy. The other is the idea of being prepared, emotionally, physically, intellectually, and spiritually, for our own potential experience.

I believe crisis gets our attention. It creates the opportunity for real and sustained change. Out of crisis greatness emerges, and the capacity for helping others increases. It heightens our ability to prepare ourselves for that eventuality and affects our decisions to shape our future by being better prepared in all aspects of our lives. We can change ourselves in subtle and not so subtle ways. The value of challenges in our lives should not be underestimated. They create the opportunity for personal growth in significant ways.

Choosing Your Future

Why would I suggest that you think about changing anything about your life?

First, because you can.

Second, it may be necessary for you to do so in order to survive.

Third, once you begin to change small or large parts of your human behavior, it opens the door to even grander changes.

Fourth, we are driven by habits and patterns that dictate much of what we do each day. Unless we are willing to change some of our habits, nothing much will change.

Fifth, by eliminating a bad habit, we can create a new and better habit that allows for our growth. It unleashes our potential and gives us the chance to grow faster.

Aristotle had it right when he said, "We are what we repeatedly do." To paraphrase Henry Ford and Albert Einstein, if we always do what we have always done, we will always get what we've always gotten. Unless we change our behavior, we will never change our results.

Lysset Butler, our vice president, is a classic example of changing the paradigm and determining her future. She came to the United States as an immigrant from Cuba at the age of eight, speaking no English. She began working immediately following high school. She rose to the top of each job she had, but she wanted more. She came to work for us fifteen years ago with a high school diploma. While working forty to sixty hours a week for us, she got her bachelor's degree in psychology and has completed her master's degree in education. Soon she may embark on studies for her PhD. She decided what her future would be. She chose to design her life and push herself to greatness, for her, within the realm of her potential. She has been a great friend, advisor, and colleague for all these many years.

Warren Rustand is one of those rare and remarkable beings, akin to Master Yoda. He has a masterful ability to convey the principles he teaches, which are genuinely transformational, direct others to a path where they can attain self-actualization and evolve to a level of transcendence. Warren's teachings are saturated with practical wisdom derived from his life experiences, as well as God-given wisdom. Warren is a mentor to mentors, a blessing to all whose lives he touches, and my dear friend.

—**Lysset Butler, Vice President, Summit Capital**

Each of us are given quiet moments of inspiration that can change our lives. Those small doses of truth, our truth, make all the difference in our lives. Sometimes we are the only ones who will ever know about them, but they shape and fashion us in ways that may only become obvious later in life. We also have quiet failures, both personally and professionally. While they may not be seen or felt by others, we know they have occurred, and we learn from them.

The idea that we can learn from times that hurt us or do damage to our self-esteem is important to our self-development. In the same way, we have periods of success that are uniquely personal. The little triumphs that lead us to bigger accomplishments. These build our self-confidence and allow us to expand our horizons and gain clarity about our future.

How then can we gain a deeper understanding of our potential for transitioning our lives and businesses from where we are to where we want to be? How do we catch this wave of transformation going on in the marketplace?

The Speed of Change

The world has always been changing at what seems to most to be a rapid pace. For many, change is incomprehensible, and for others it is easily understood. However, we are now seeing the world evolving at an ever-increasing speed, exponentially greater speed. Leaders, and businesses, must change at a pace consistent with the speed at which the world is changing, or both will be a footnote in history. Those who ignore this change will likely be washed away in the early waves of transition and transformation.

Leaders, and their leadership, must change at the same exponential rate. Their failure to do so will relegate them to a position of always trying to catch up to those that have kept pace. Entrepreneurs and entrepreneurial companies have the greatest capacity to adapt to the new world. They tend to be more agile and mobile, with the ability to adapt both in leadership and within their business.

I want to share a way of thinking about what knowledge and principles allow us to adapt most quickly and how we can apply them to our family, business, community, and self. The very same principles and understandings will give us the edge to learn ourselves, teach others, and create more leaders who will make our organizations stronger and more vibrant.

So, what is happening in the marketplace right now? Businesses are moving from being content, product, or service providers into growing platforms and beyond. The world is becoming one global supermarket, where people choose to shop at a few places like Amazon, the Apple Store, or Facebook, as these places provide an easy purchase, access to almost unlimited choices, and curation based on a customer's personal preferences.

Standing out is possible if a company has a strong brand, creates a social bond, provides a unique experience, or offers personalized products and services. Business dynamics center around information, platforms, and impact, which also drive revenues. Businesses must have a leader, and leaders, who can make a business adaptable, connected to major platforms, measurable, and programmatic. Can you and your team evolve your company at the current pace of change?

Which leadership principles can allow an entrepreneur to be successful and build other leaders and their company? I would offer the ones that have, at their core, the capacity to adapt, connect, measure, impact, and program for future success. Basically, those leadership principles that stay intact during changes and transitions in the business environment and work as the DNA in every circumstance for the individual and their companies. It is the predictable and consistent application of those principles that will give certainty to the ever-evolving climate of change.

While some people feel they have managed to master their lives, others might feel that they have just barely touched the surface of their potential. Both can be correct; in any case the responsibility and accountability for our lives is our own.

The Evolution of Leadership

For several years I have had the privilege of mentoring two wonderfully talented women, Natalia Matveeva and Mary Leonida. As I talked with each, privately, I came to have great respect for their unique gifts and talents. They pursued very different paths but both very successfully. Both have personal experience in applying the principles herein discussed, and as a result their lives have been permanently altered.

We hosted twenty leaders at our home, including Natalia and Mary, who had traveled great distances to talk about how to advance these concepts to a larger audience. A plan was created and is being executed.

During this meeting and after, my two great friends made a significant contribution to our thinking on this subject. Natalia (her story is in Chapter 7) and Mary (her story is in Chapter 8) have added their voices and thoughts to our consideration of leadership principles. Natalia, specifically, suggested that my definition of life by design would fit well with Maslow's hierarchy of needs. As she and I exchanged thoughts on this, it became evident that she was right. Therefore, I want to give her credit for her thoughts and writing. The following part was cowritten and designed by Natalia.

Evolution starts with self.

One of the theories that seeks to explain the leadership evolution of self was proposed by Abraham Maslow. According to the Maslow hierarchy of needs, there are six levels. The first four levels are those at which most people live and operate. Those who make it to the fifth and sixth levels are there not by coincidence but rather through striving and stretching for their higher being.

·e what Maslow was talking about by revising the

ls.

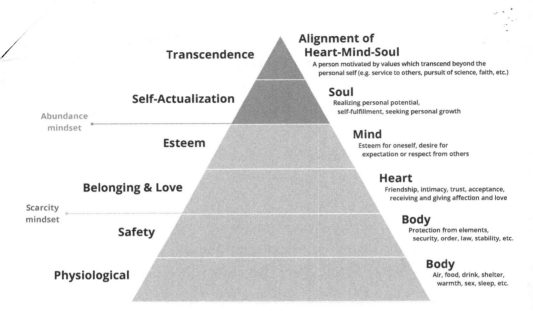

The first two levels cover the physiological and safety needs, and to simplify we will call them the body levels, as they refer to the food, air, warmth, shelter, security, and so forth that are needed for a human body to survive. These levels are achievable for most people in their current state.

After the first two levels are met, then the third level naturally develops, and we would call this the heart level, or belonging and love. A human being is a social creature and in order to survive and develop properly, one needs friendship, intimacy, trust, and acceptance, receiving and giving affection and love.

The fourth level is self-esteem, or the mind level. After a person has met their basic needs in levels one through three, one moves to achieving a reputation and developing respect for, and interaction with, others. Indicators of this level are self-esteem, self-worth, a sense of well-being. This requires intentionality.

Next comes the fifth level, which is self-actualization. We may call it the soul level. This is when a person is seeking personal growth and self-fulfillment as an end in itself. It is the notion of achieving a high level of individual potential and development.

The original Maslow hierarchy had this as the highest level. However, late in his career, Maslow added a sixth level known as transcendence. While he may not have had the opportunity to develop this fully, this is the level beyond oneself. It is a place where one thinks of the welfare and benefit of others. Serving the greater good becomes the prime motivation.

This is the higher calling for one's life. This is the level at which the heart, mind, and soul are aligned. Decision-making is based on core values and driven by intentionality rather than circumstances. What moves someone to the top of the Maslow hierarchy is vision, intent, and values, coupled with the alignment of heart, mind, and soul.

Clarity of vision is a process by which the alignment of heart, mind, and soul, joined by intentionality and values, are integrated for the purpose of making future choices and decisions. Clarity of vision serves as a platform for one's future life.

—Warren Rustand

How does one get clarity of vision? Further on in the book, you will read much more about it and its application so that you can use it effectively. We are suggesting a purposeful design that will be helpful and widely applicable. For now may I suggest that one's life purpose is based on a trinity of:

1. clarity of vision

2. certainty of intent

3. power of values

These penetrate every level of Maslow's expanded hierarchy of needs and every aspect of one's life.

Consciously or subconsciously every person makes decisions based on their vision, intent, and values. The entrepreneurial leader brings to the company his or her own set of all three. When the company's vision, intent, and values reflect those of the founder or leader, he or she is more motivated and driven to overcome challenges that any business encounters, as the very purpose of the company's existence reflects that of the entrepreneur's life.

The same happens when a family is created and two partners bring different perspectives and life experiences into their partnership or marriage. They are happy to support each other and invest in the relationship when they have a common vision, intent, and values. When there is no alignment, it can cause conflict and difficulties.

It is clear that the platform can be expanded into all areas of one's life. It creates a framework for our family, business, community, and personal growth and development. Our inner compass already knows what we want, how we want to live, and what outcomes we desire.

As Maslow suggests, one can level up from one area to another. By the alignment of heart, mind, and soul into all levels of Maslow's hierarchy, one begins to understand the opportunity to alter the course of one's life in all areas of application.

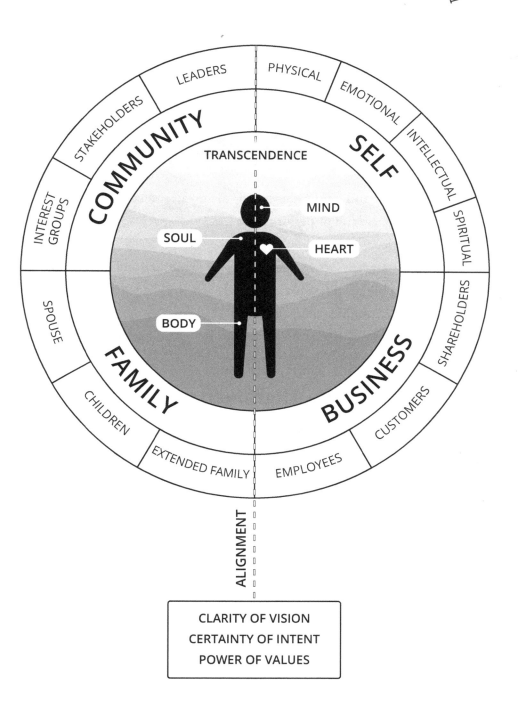

This drawing illustrates a life platform or framework. The foundation holds the key principles that give life purpose and motivational energy. This allows one to move from satisfying basic needs (body) to reaching the growth needs (soul), thus enabling one to achieve the higher vision, which allows one to achieve transcendence, where heart, mind, and soul are aligned and work in tandem to realize one's highest potential.

The larger and clearer the vision, the greater the opportunity to achieve a higher level of performance.

Vision feeds motivation.

Motivation helps to overcome obstacles to learning and succeeding.

Success builds self-esteem.

Self-esteem builds one's potential.

And potential, once realized, builds the greater good.

Discovering the Alignment: The Story of Winnie Hart

At 6:10 a.m. on Monday, August 29, 2005, Hurricane Katrina made landfall in Louisiana. The levees broke, and more than 80 percent of the city was flooded with more than 224 billion gallons of water. Winnie lost 75 percent of her business in a weekend. Before that day she thought that failure was the worst possible thing that could happen. She learned what would become her mantra: From crisis comes opportunity. From failure she learned resilience. From failure she learned that a strong vision sees no barriers.

The collapse of her Louisiana business forced her to align her business ambitions with her purpose. When your purpose is in alignment with what you stand for, you are connected to who you are meant to be. What you stand for shapes the impact you have on the world and makes the difference between building a company that is ordinary and building one that is extraordinary.

Being a naturally optimistic person, and having the name Hart, she was bound to find opportunity in crisis. She began to rebuild her business, moving part of it to Houston, Texas, and continuing to rebuild her business in New Orleans. She also engaged in a personal journey of discovery by the pursuit of clarity of vision. When she found that, she also realized that the tragedy and failure prompted by Katrina were actually gifts. Her struggles were being rewarded with greater insight. She became quite focused on her certainty of intent as she executed her plans and published her first book, *Stand Out: Tools to Master the 8 Fundamentals of Standing Out in Business.*

She wrote her second book, *What Do You Stand For?*, to guide others in discovering what they stand for and the difference they make in the world, and she returned the gift to the organization from which she had received such help and comfort during her trials. She has become a leading servant leader for EO, serving in numerous leadership positions, and now is a member of its global board of directors. She is serving others as she was served. I am honored to be her friend and feel the strength of her being, for she has created the alignment of heart, mind, and soul through her clarity of vision.

We all have a leader within us that has the potential to achieve our highest purpose. Warren's inspiration and guidance empowered me to discover mine: to guide leaders to discover their purpose so that they can make a difference in the world. This book is the leadership guide we all need to tap into our unique purpose and build a life with intent supported by enduring values. Now more than ever, our world depends on it.

—Winnie Hart, Author, Speaker, Board
Director, Founder of TwinEngine

Overcoming the Dream Killer

Throughout these pages I want to educate and entertain you, but my ultimate goal is to give you a factual, accurate, and unassuming look at my life and what I have learned along the way. Some things in my life have come through deliberate choice. Some things have happened purely by chance. But I hope my story can inspire you to take action. It is not going to do you any good to read what I've written, then close the book, shrug your shoulders, put it on a shelf, and say, "That was nice." The change comes when you apply these principles and this knowledge to your own life.

We have the capacity and the ability to make all the choices necessary to live the life we want to live. We can't always know what that life is going to hand us on any given day, but if we pursue these principles and apply them, we will have a fuller, richer life, and we will have more time to do the things we enjoy with those we love.

As we begin I want to address the most common dream killer so you can immediately be on the lookout. It only consists of *seven words*, yet these seven words have thwarted more goals and stalled more comebacks than probably anything else. In fact, this dream killer is so common that I'm certain you've done it, and said it, multiple times in your life. Maybe even multiple times this month.

When standing in the foothills of your dreams, which is the vision for your new life, what you're going to be tempted to do when you wake up in the morning is hit snooze. You're going to want to roll over and say, "I don't feel like doing it today." But don't succumb to this dream killer. That's the worst thing you can do.

If you were one of the people who read that, rolled your eyes, and thought, Really? Staying in bed an extra nine minutes is going to derail my entire dream?

Have you achieved that dream yet?

Thought so.

What it all comes down to is "a matter of conscious choice and discipline," exactly what Jim Collins said.

An old adage tells us that there are two kinds of people who get up in the morning: those who jump out of bed and say, "Good morning, Lord!" and are ready for the challenge of the new day and those who peek out from under the covers and grumble, "Good Lord, it's morning."

Some days you are going to jump out of bed and be on fire for your future, an unstoppable force. But there will be other days, especially at the start of the journey, where you feel like doing anything but getting up early and working the process day after day, week after week. Your body will tell you that you need one more hour of sleep. But you must take control of your mind if you want a different outcome than what you've always had.

We choose how we face each day. We can be energetic, enthusiastic, upbeat, optimistic, happy, or we can be grumpy, sour, critical, and sarcastic. But we control our mind. We can't blame others for how we're feeling and how we're thinking. We can't point at others and say they made me feel sad or they made me unhappy or they hurt my feelings. We choose how we react to others, and so, as a result of that, we do control our mind and what we think—and how we think is who we are. What we think is what we'll be. Our thoughts really matter, so each day we need to control our thoughts to the greatest degree possible.

No one is making you unhappy; no one is making you sad; no one's causing you not to be successful. No one is choosing to keep you from opportunities. These are choices that we make with our mind every day, so be aware and be certain that you control your mind and live the life you want to live.

This quote of mine is important to your future. "Success is relevant only when measured against one's own potential." Your success is only relevant to you, based on your potential. It has nothing to do with me. Likewise, my success and my potential have nothing to do with anyone else.

To be clear, your different outcomes have nothing to do with comparing yourself to or against others. We will never win the comparison race. Someone is always better looking, better dressed, or better educated; someone will always have a faster car, a bigger home, more money, or less body fat. I can't win that game, and neither can you, but I can win the game of understanding *my* potential and measuring myself against that potential. This should be your goal every day. Every. Single. Day.

Here's where I'll offer some tough love. And I am saying this as sincerely as I can because I've had this same talk with myself many times: Who cares if you don't feel like doing it today?

It doesn't matter if you don't feel like doing it.

It only matters *if* you do it because nobody cares about your dream as much as you do.

Tomorrow morning you might roll over and think, *I don't want to do meal prep today. I'll just grab fast food at lunchtime. Right now, I just want more sleep.* Fast food might keep you full for an hour or two, but is it helping you achieve your fitness goals so you can be more active with your kids?

You might get up next Tuesday and say, "I don't feel like training for the half-marathon today." Well, the only person the decision to train or not is going to affect is *you* when you go run the half-marathon. Do you want to give it your best? Or are you okay with a subpar performance because you didn't stick to the training schedule? If you want to climb Mount Everest but don't want to prepare and train, that's fine, but you dramatically increase your risk.

Assuming your goal isn't a life-or-death matter, who cares what you *feel* like? If you want to perform, if you want to be your best, if you want to do your best, then you have to consistently do the things that will take you to the finish line. You have to stick with the process, even when you don't want to. No excuses.

In the end nobody cares whether you feel like doing it today or not. It only matters *if* you do it.

The world is not changed by those who *feel*.

The world is changed by those who *do*.

PART I

THE THREE PRINCIPLES OF LEADERSHIP

The genius of man is not that he can remake the world, but rather that he can remake himself.

—Mahatma Gandhi

There are three principles of leadership that I have practiced and observed in others that are applied almost universally by people that you and I might say are exceptional or extraordinary. Remember, the three principles are:

Clarity of vision

Certainty of intent

Power of values

These are the three pillars of what I call "life by design." This is something I have been teaching others for forty years and practicing myself for all of my adult life—these are the ideas of knowing where you are going, directionally or specifically, what you are going to do to get there, and what your behavior will be on your journey.

People from different nationalities, cultures, ethnicities, and ɪgions all over the world have now applied these principles and have had remarkable success. These three principles very easily apply to all areas of one's life, whether it is family, business, community, or self. These three principles assist you in creating the right mindset of increased performance in every aspect of your life. There is a pattern of success, and when principles are applied in a particular way, it increases and enhances the chance for success.

These principles are designed to simplify our lives, not to make them more complex. It takes our integrity and adherence to these life principles to change our outcomes.

CHAPTER 2

PRINCIPLE OF LEADERSHIP NUMBER ONE: CLARITY OF VISION

Some see but have no vision. Some hear but have no understanding.

When I graduated from high school, I was one of the commencement speakers. When I confidently walked down off that stage, ready to head off to the big senior party, my father stopped me. He had a piece of paper in his hand, and he said, "Well, you've done well in high school; what do you plan on doing in college?" He was very straightforward with me; to be successful, now was the time I needed to have vision about my future.

Of course I was anxious to get going and have fun, so I quickly rattled off a few things. I wanted to be an all-American basketball player, student body president at the University of Arizona, the outstanding graduate, a Rhodes Scholar, and be inducted into Phi Beta Kappa, the academic honor society. As I spoke my father wrote down my goals on that sheet of paper and then handed it to me. "Please sign this," he said. So, I signed it and went on my way.

Now I was young and mostly naïve about what would come next, but this was my first real experience with clarity of vision. The simple act of choosing, making a concrete and specific decision about what I wanted to do in college, shaped the way I saw my future. This simple act helped me see more clearly what I needed to do in college. It gave me direction and specific challenges. Now I had something real to move toward, and I was committed. My father was proving a point, and I knew I'd see that piece of paper again.

> We should seek clarity of vision in everything we do. With clarity we can be much more efficient and effective in all things, large or small.

We should seek clarity of vision in everything we do. With clarity we can be much more efficient and effective in all things, large or small. When we are asked, or decide to do, something, why not take the time to think it through very carefully, seeking clarity? Perhaps we are asked to chair a committee, lead a fundraiser, or coach a team, or we decide to get a degree, or take a new job, get married and raise a family, or climb Mount Everest. Each commitment requires us to think it through—all the ramifications, subtleties, and nuances. As we do this, we will invariably be better in everything we do.

Clarity Has No Restrictions: The Story of Jamie Douraghy

Most great leaders know where they are going; their successes unwaveringly come after a great deal of hard work, sacrifice, dedication, and alignment with their vision. We can only be as successful as our vision is clear. We should seek clarity of vision in the smallest and largest choices we make. The clearer our vision, the easier it is to act with intent. It is the distant landmark against which we measure our progress.

Let me tell you a story about one of our granddaughters, Connor. From a very young age, she knew that she wanted to be a pediatrician. Often children have aspirations at a young age, but hers was very specific and never wavered. Although she (along with all our grandchildren, of course) excels at a variety of activities and skills, she made that decision as a young child and began to act on that decision. She has just completed her undergraduate degree and is studying to take the MCAT, which will help determine what medical school she will attend. Her vision was clear, even from childhood, and with that clarity came a path she took one step at a time. I have no doubt that she will succeed because she made specific choices based on her clarity of vision.

Not all of us are born with that innate desire to follow a specific dream or career path; we often end up where we are through chance, serendipity, or luck because of circumstances beyond our control. We don't necessarily have a design for our life because we haven't grasped that clarity of vision. But we can decide to change at any age.

In December of 2011, I gave a speech about human potential in Los Angeles to about two hundred CEOs and their spouses. After the talk a man came up to me and introduced himself as Jamie Douraghy, CEO of Artisan Creative. He said he wanted to win the US veteran fencing championships. I was a bit surprised, but curious, and I asked him if he'd ever fenced before.

He went on to tell me that he'd fenced most of his life, through his teens and twenties, before getting married and starting a business. He competed, sometimes seriously, sometimes not so seriously, and he was at the point where he really wanted to get to the next level. He had won championships along the way, had reached a plateau and couldn't get beyond it. I could tell this man had found his clarity of vision, the US championship. His goal was specific, and he seemed willing to get to work; he just needed to figure out the next few steps.

"How old are you, Jamie?" I asked.

"Fifty-two," he said. I'm not an expert in fencing, but I hadn't heard of many athletes who had three decades of competition and then decided to become world-class in their field. I told him as much, but he was determined. I agreed to work with him on one condition: that he would follow my lead and do everything I asked of him. He said that he would, but I confess I had my doubts. I asked him to call me early the next week if he was still committed. Lo and behold, early Monday the phone rang.

"This is Jamie Douraghy, and I want to be the US veteran fencing champion," he said.

So, we got to work.

We started working together on January 1, 2012, and Jamie, true to his word, did everything I asked him to do. We began to rebuild his competitive life psychologically, emotionally, and physically. He got a new fencing coach. I coached him on areas of discipline, consistency, and the psychology of winning. Additionally, we spent considerable time on family, business, community, and self. And in that process, he began to see things changing in his entire life. He changed his mindset. Six months and twenty-five days later, I flew to Los Angeles and went to the Anaheim convention center, where the USA Fencing National Championships were being held. Jamie was one of sixty fencers who had qualified for the national championships. Jamie's wife, Katty, and I sat, watched, and cheered for him as he worked his way through a series of twelve matches.

At the close of that long day, Jamie was competing for the gold medal to become the US veteran national champion. While he lost that match 10–9, he learned a lot about himself and what he was capable of doing. Since then Jamie has won several veterans' championships.

He's been on seven US teams that have gone to the Veterans Fencing World Championships. In October of 2019, he competed again for the world championship in Cairo, Egypt, where he took the bronze medal individually and led his US team to their first-ever silver medal.

Jamie's clarity of vision was the first step, the catalyst. The second step was to change his mindset, and then his dreams came true. He intentionally acted on his vision every day.

Warren's writings are more than just words on pages; they are the blueprint of how he lives his life and the principles he has embodied for many years. We have learned much from Warren as a mentor and friend, both individually and as a couple, as he consistently encouraged us to push past our limiting beliefs and discover new heights. When we first read The Leader within Us, *it was interesting to see the many pages we had each highlighted and dog-eared; there was so much to learn and apply! We discussed the many key points and aligned around how to best design a life that follows his eight principles of leadership, which start with oneself.*

—Jamie and Katty Douraghy, Cofounders
   of Life Work Integration

Three Steps to Developing Clarity

It should be no surprise that the process required to develop clarity of vision takes both time and space. Specifically, there are three steps required to develop clarity.

The first thing we need to do is **separate ourselves from our busyness and find time and space to think;** physical and mental space are the keys. Quiet the mind. If you have a crazy schedule at work, either take some time off and get away or take a weekend to yourself. If you have a full family schedule, carve out some time each night for a week or two so you can really focus on your vision. Finding the time might prove difficult, but even if it means getting up thirty minutes earlier to have a few moments of peace and quiet, it will pay off in a big way later. Do not think it is easy to find your vision but rather expect to struggle with it a bit to find the clarity you seek.

My life usually moves along at a fast clip; I have to make time in my daily work schedule to focus on my vision because there is often no other option. Over the years I have found a routine that works for me. Every day at 10:00 a.m. and again at 2:00 p.m., for one hour each time, I clear my schedule, shut my door, turn off my technology, and take a moment to think deeply about what I'm doing and where I'm going. One day I might be thinking about clarity of vision regarding a business strategy. The next day I may use the time to mull over a family goal or vision and how to work toward it. Some days, if I have a little more flexibility, I'll drive up to the mountains near my home and just think. No matter where I am, I consistently find the time to do this exercise. I have worked hard to incorporate this routine into my daily life, and I have seen the benefits time and time again. The key is to dedicate your time, without interruption, regularly and consistently. Then focus on the clarity you seek.

The second step in developing clarity is for us to write down where we're going and what exactly we want to do. When I was nineteen years old, I wrote a list of one hundred things I wanted to accomplish in my lifetime. Some were soft and easy, but others were complex and difficult (I'll talk more about the top one hundred list in Chapter 8). It is amazing what we can achieve if we just set our goals and work at them.

We have the luxury of deciding what we want to do in our lifetime.

When we physically write our goals down so the eye sees something written, our minds retain them longer. The words leave a more indelible impression than if we just think about what we'd like to accomplish. Technology is great, but if you can, create a handwritten list so you are physically transferring your desires onto the page.

The third step is to determine our purpose. The very reason we do what we do. To discern and discover our purpose is to give greater meaning and commitment to our lives. This is so important, for individuals, families, and businesses. For me, family has always been a catalyst, a driving force, my clarity and my purpose. Over the years we have tried to keep our family vision at the forefront of every decision.

This is our family vision statement: "An eternally sealed family that helps each member reach their potential through unconditional love and respect for differences, in which all are committed to lead Christ-centered lives, and that serves as a protective shield for all within."

Knowing *why* we're doing something always helps us make progress. Remembering our vision in times of frustration or difficulty can often save us from giving up or falling back on those familiar patterns that keep us comfortable yet stuck. A common saying in gyms and with personal trainers is "When you feel like giving up, remember why you started." A brief moment of distraction and contemplation is often all it takes to refocus our efforts and get to work.

The Story of Reza Bavar

It's 2010, and I've just delivered a speech at a conference in Jeddah, Saudi Arabia. After my speech I saw a young man, who I believed was probably forty years old (I would later learn he was only thirty-four), standing shyly in a line of people who were discussing the talk.

I soon had the opportunity to meet him; he introduced himself as Reza Bavar. His outward appearance didn't initially portray confidence or success. He was quite overweight, had wrinkled clothes and long, unkempt hair, and was unshaven. He shared that he was living a very unhealthy lifestyle with excessive food, alcohol, and sleep coupled with no real exercise or discipline in his life. As I began to learn about Reza, I understood why he was unhappy and, as he later confided to me, suicidal.

Reza was an immigrant from Iran. He was a lawyer by training and owned his own law firm, but he didn't enjoy his business and wanted a change. He dreamed of creating beautiful consumer products and planned to embark on his dream by making specialty hookah pipes, which were one of his passions at that time. Despite his dream, the reality was that Reza lived in almost constant fear of the financial health of his law firm and a mountain of debt he had accumulated through a frivolous lifestyle. In truth, Reza had already committed acts out of desperation born of his fears that would later get him disbarred in California. He could no longer deny the damage he was doing to his business and his physical health through his self-destructive choices and habits. He wanted to become healthier, start a new business, find a partner in life, start a family, and live a life founded on humility, integrity, and courage—traits that were dormant in Reza in 2010.

About a year after our first meeting, I began to mentor Reza, and we became very close friends. As we worked together, he found a clarity of vision, and we began to incorporate new and different actions that would strengthen every aspect of his life. Reza was developing a vision for his life that was very different than the life he was leading. I believed in him and in his dreams and was willing to hold him accountable to become the person I knew was struggling to break free of the hellish existence he was trapped in. Reza needed to do the work to achieve his dreams, and he dedicated himself to living out the principles I was teaching him and that he knew were true.

Reza began exercising; he went jogging every morning and reengaged with his yoga practice, something he had abandoned as he lost focus on the vision he had set for his life. In short order, he went from waking up at 11:00 a.m. to waking up before dawn to run and, within one month, he was able to run eight miles. He began to take pride in his appearance and slowly started to let go of illusory fears that had been holding him back from the life he wanted and deserved. It took incredible sacrifice, but through intense focus and effort, Reza began a manufacturing business building hookah pipes.

Six months after we started working together, Reza was leading a conference for about four hundred EOers from the Western United States called EO Alchemy. Many of Reza's friends and acquaintances hadn't seen him since we had started working with each other, and when he walked on stage to begin the conference, there was an audible gasp from some of those who had known him for a long time but hadn't seen him in person for a while. He looked like he'd walked out of *GQ* magazine; his appearance and mindset were totally different. Well, what had transpired?

In deciding to make the change, he started with his physical capacity and then added emotional, intellectual, and spiritual capacity to his transformation—his own personal alchemy. Reza lost, and kept off, fifty pounds, deepened his yoga practice and even became a yoga teacher, cut his hair, changed his wardrobe, closed his law practice, and opened his manufacturing company.

Today he is a fit, exceptional CEO of a fast-growing company, preparing to birth another incredible venture. He travels the globe, has paid off nearly all of his debt, has a special lady in his life, and is in the process of applying for reinstatement to the State Bar of California.

His family is stronger, he is stronger, and he's a blessing to the lives of others through his particular talents and gifts as a coach and a mentor.

It is not easy at first, but anyone can make the changes Reza did if they are committed, if they have discipline, and if they base those changes on specific principles.

I have had the privilege of knowing Warren for a decade now. I have personally witnessed the impeccable quality of his character and transformational leadership style, and because of that, Warren has been an extraordinary force for good in my life. I consider the wisdom encapsulated in Warren's book to be invaluable, and for the brave souls truly committed to the path of self-actualization, it will be a priceless tool in that journey.

—**Reza Bavar, CEO and Founder, Kaloud, Inc.**

Protecting the Dream

Clarity of vision affects every part of our lives, and we must protect it at all costs. That means not only protecting the time we take to consistently seek and grow our vision but also taking care in sharing our vision with others, especially if they won't support us on the journey or don't believe we have the ability to achieve our vision. There's enough negativity in the world; don't allow another person's pessimism to creep into your vision. Hold strong and press forward anyway, even when you're the only person who believes in your vision. If you can surround yourself with people who *do* support you and believe in you, even better.

In my teenage years I was a good high school basketball player. Still, there were many who told me I didn't have the body or ability to play college basketball. I was six-two, but some thought I wasn't tall enough. Instead of holding me back, their words inspired my clarity of vision. I had a vision of being a student leader, academically strong, and a good college basketball player. My vision drove me.

I attended the University of Arizona from 1961 to 1965. I was student body president, Arizona's first-ever Academic All-American, all-conference for three years, and Arizona's outstanding graduate. I enjoyed the actualization of my vision.

Following my senior year, I was drafted in 1965 by the San Francisco Warriors, now the Golden State Warriors. I believe I was the thirtieth draft choice that year.

Now, there were fewer NBA teams at that time, fewer NBA players, but it was still a unique opportunity. Alex Hannum, a big old burly ex-NBA player, was the coach, and they had some great players: Nate Thurmond, Tom Meschery, Al Attles, Rick Barry. I was with some elite players.

After I had been working out rigorously with the team, Coach Hannum came to me one day and said, "You know, Warren, there are three things you have to have to be a great professional basketball player."

And I said, "Coach, I'd like to be a great professional basketball player. What are those three things?"

"First, you have to be intelligent, you have to understand the offense, the defense, the transitions, the matchups, all the things we are trying to accomplish, and you score high there."

I said, "Thank you. What's the second one?"

"The second one is that you have to give us maximum effort each time you're out, meaning that you have to really play hard because all these athletes are great athletes; they all want to win. Everyone wants to do well, and therefore how you compete day in, day out matters.

You score high on effort, too."

I said, "Thank you, Coach."

He said, "You're just missing one of the three great qualities of being a great professional basketball player."

I said, "Coach, I've wanted to be a great professional basketball player for a while. Now what is it I'm missing?"

"Talent," he chuckled.

The next year I played for the Phillips 66ers, the number-one AAU basketball team in the United States. We played for a national championship that year and were beaten in the finals by Cazzie Russell, the great All-American, and his teammates from Michigan, who assembled to play in that national championship tournament.

Shortly thereafter I was selected to play on the US team for the 1966 World Basketball Championships in Santiago, Chile, where we won the silver medal. We lost by a handful of points to Yugoslavia, but it was a great learning experience, except that I contracted typhoid fever the last few days in Santiago and had to be flown back to the States and hospitalized for two weeks. Again, I was following my boyhood vision, and it allowed me to contribute my best to my team.

I am not special, as Coach Hannum let me know, but I had a vision and a talent I nurtured, and my persistence led me to play basketball. Then it led me to the White House, and then to sitting on boards of directors and to leading numerous companies.

If you're thinking that's uncommon for someone with my ability and skill, you're right. Because I'm really quite an average person. But this is just one example of what you can do once you decide on a clarity of vision, take the necessary steps to intentionally reach your goal, and surround yourself with people who support you.

Never Too Late

You might be wondering if your age has any bearing on your dreams. Is it ever too soon or too late to develop our clarity of vision and start working toward our goals? Not at all. My granddaughter had clarity of vision as a young child. And Jamie Douraghy didn't begin to fully act on his vision until he was fifty-two years old. As long as we continue to search and don't give up, our goals are possible at any age.

There are many people who didn't reach the pinnacle of their success until their sixties or seventies. Some award-winning authors didn't start writing until their seventies. And there are politicians who weren't elected until late in life. There are many examples of people who have found remarkable success, both in public and private, for their visions at different times of their lives. Every person has the opportunity to find their personal greatness in quiet moments of success.

Another question I'm often asked is whether everyone has something special within them. Do I really think that everyone on this beautiful earth has something special—some gift or talent or desire or purpose? The answer is yes, I really do believe it. Every person ever born has the potential to do something uniquely great. Whether it impacts a few, hundreds, or thousands isn't what's important. It's what you do with the gifts and capacities you have been given or have cultivated that matters.

Once we discover our vision and purpose, we're unstoppable. I've seen it happen time and time again, because our dreams don't require a certain genetic makeup or a specific talent or physical body—factors we can't control. The stories of people who have accomplished great things and who have overcome a great deal are largely stories of people who have decided to change their life because they wanted something else, something different, or something more than what they had previously known. They made a *mindset* change, and then they employed a specific discipline to make the *life* change.

Clarity of vision is our true north. It is nothing without the work and determination that follows it, but it boldly leads us and our lives toward something special.

TLC Case Study: Clarity of Vision

In 1993 I received a call from a good friend of mine, Gary Jonas, who lived in Washington, DC. We had been friends for a long time, traveled the world together, and had a lot of fun. I knew he was smart, diligent, and detailed. On the call he was explaining to me that he believed that someday doctors would operate on the human eye using lasers and other advanced techniques. I pushed back, saying I didn't think that would happen because ophthalmologists and optometrists would want to keep control of the patients, and they would never give up the ability to operate on the eye, as ophthalmologists did.

Undeterred by my disbelief, he continued his discussions with me, continued his own research, and became more convincing. Six months later a group of us came together to invest, raise money, and begin the process of building a company.

At the time, the US Food and Drug Administration had not approved the process, but Canada and other countries had. We had the opportunity to open a clinic in Toronto, working with doctors and patients from both the United States and Canada. We began to build our knowledge of this space.

When the FDA did approve this technique, we were one of the first companies, if not *the* first company, to begin to open clinics in the United States. We recruited doctors from all over the United States, traveling to the various urban areas where we wanted to have clinics, and we sought out the very best doctors. We did our research in those communities, finding out who had the best reputations, the best and most successful practices, the most training. And we would meet with those doctors and talk to them about our vision for building a LASIK eye surgery company. Many of them signed on and agreed to work with us.

About that time we became aware of a small Canadian public company that was in the same business, and we thought it appropriate to merge with them and become a public company on the Toronto Stock Exchange, which we did. The resulting company was known as TLC Vision, and it became the largest LASIK eye surgery company in the world.

We built a wonderful public company with a great corporate culture. Thousands of doctors practiced in hundreds of sites where patients would go to have eye surgery. Millions of patients today have better eyesight as a result of the vision of a few.

I was on the board of directors. Elias Vamvakas was the visionary leader and CEO, and Gary Jonas was the chief operating officer, responsible for driving the business on a day-to-day basis and creating the culture that was so successful for the business. Gary gave much to his family, friends, and colleagues. He is missed by all.

When the recession of 2008 hit, elective, cash-only surgery dried up. Total eye procedures were cut in half, and so we had to downsize the company. I became chairman and interim CEO. It was necessary to take the company through bankruptcy, which was a very challenging time. It was ultimately taken private with a private equity group. TLC Vision remains a powerful company in the LASIK eye surgery business.

Swift Ships Case Study: Clarity of Vision

After leaving the White House near the end of the Ford administration, my college roommate, Bill Nicholson, my friends Joe Mermis and Ed Sampson, and I began to look around for an entrepreneurial opportunity. We found such an opportunity in a small company in Morgan City, Louisiana, called Swift Ships.

Swift Ships is a company that had built aluminum-hulled riverboats for the Vietnam conflict, some 225 boats, twenty-caliber machine guns fore and aft. They would patrol the Mekong Delta and other waterways to assist the US military with their operations during the Vietnam War.

At the time we met the owners, they were building cargo, crew, and utility boats for the offshore oil platforms. We borrowed the money from some good friends, Jay Van Andel and Rich DeVos, who owned Amway.

Assisted by New York Bank, we acquired Swift Ships. And while we didn't know anything about building those kinds of boats, we had a keen interest in learning. So, we spent the necessary time to get up to speed on the manufacturing process for the boats.

We retained the senior management team, added Bill Nicholson as the operating partner, and began building the company. We had a clear vision for what we thought the company could be, and with that clarity of vision we began to exercise certainty of intent in building the company.

Our time in Washington, DC, and the White House was a classic opportunity for us to use our knowledge of what would happen when the countries in the Middle East formed the oil cartel, which would limit production and drive prices up. The United States would move toward energy independence; when they moved toward energy independence, they would need the very boats that we were making to support the offshore oil platforms that were being developed. So, as a result of that, we had very strong growth in the company that we acquired.

We sold that company some six years later for a tenfold return on our investment. It was a wonderful experience and one in which knowing public policy, oil production, and understanding America's quest for energy independence allowed us to build a company that we otherwise would not have been able to build.

Health Equity Case Study: Clarity of Vision

I was approached several years ago by three young men—Steve Neeleman, David Hall, and Nuno Battaglia—who had an idea for creating a company that focused on HSAs (health savings accounts) as an alternative to the traditional employer-owned or government-offered insurance programs. It's simply a process of individual savings accounts to be applied to healthcare when needed.

They had a vision and asked if I would be the founding chairman of the board. The first meetings were in the basement of our home, before subsequently moving to an office, raising capital, and doing all the other necessary start-up activities.

They were always driving toward the vision of creating an alternative to traditional healthcare. And in that process, to their credit, they built an extraordinary business called Health Equity, which is today the second- or third-largest HSA company in the United States.

They moved the business from Tucson to Salt Lake City, ultimately took the company public, and it has had a very substantial gain. But the leadership that got it to that point was all about the clarity of vision and then the intentionality of execution.

The List Reappears: Lessons in Achievement from My Father

Remember that piece of paper from the beginning of the chapter? It turned up again.

When I graduated from high school, I was one of the commencement speakers. As I walked down from the stage, I was surprised to see my father with a paper and pen in his hand. He said, "You have done well. Now what are you going to do at the University of Arizona?"

I was anxious to go out with my friends, so I listed five quick things that I wanted to achieve: All-American basketball player, student body president, outstanding graduate in my class, Rhodes Scholar, and Phi Beta Kappa. He wrote each down, asked me to sign it, and said to have a good time that night with my friends.

That piece of paper from my father turned up again four years later, when I graduated from the University of Arizona. Once again I was on the commencement stage, and when I finished and walked down the steps, I was surprised to see my father with paper and pen in his hand, ready to assess where my clarity of vision had taken me.

He opened the paper, and on it were the five things I had written down four years earlier as I had graduated from high school. Then he drew a line next to the five items on the list from four years prior (all-American basketball player, student body president, outstanding graduate, a Rhodes Scholar, and Phi Beta Kappa) and he wrote *success* on one heading and *failure* on the other. And then he went down the list, checking off each item.

He then asked me, "Were you an All-American basketball player?"
I said, "Yes," and he marked *success.*
He asked, "Were you student body president?"
I said, "Yes," and he marked *success.*

"Were you the outstanding graduate in your class based on character and leadership?"

"Yes." He marked *success.*

"Were you a Rhodes Scholar?"

"Well, I wanted to be a Rhodes Scholar, and I was competing, but you can't be married and be a Rhodes Scholar [at least at that time], and Carson and I got married. So, no."

He marked *failure.*

"Were you Phi Beta Kappa?"

"Dad, do you remember that one bad semester I had that—"

"Were you Phi Beta Kappa?"

I said, "No," and he marked *failure.*

Of the five goals I had established, I had achieved only three. I had still achieved more successes than failures, but it was a stark reminder that creating a vision and intentionally acting on that vision is critically important.

The list I had quickly rattled off at high school graduation had become the focus for my subsequent four years. Having that list in the back of my mind and knowing that my father also knew what I was working toward taught me a great deal about moving toward that vision and acting intentionally.

This process that came from my father had a lasting and indelible imprint on me. The lesson for me was, set high goals, work hard, and achieve all that you are capable of achieving.

Now that I had graduated from the University of Arizona, I knew I wanted more of that success. I now had a clear vision and better understanding of how to achieve it.

CHAPTER 3

PRINCIPLE OF LEADERSHIP NUMBER TWO: CERTAINTY OF INTENT

Better never stops. Be happy, but not satisfied.

—Sir Graham Henry

Certainty of intent naturally follows clarity of vision and is the notion that once we know where we are going, intent governs what we actually do. In other words, our vision governs our intentional actions.

Jamie Clarke's goal was to climb Mount Everest by the time he was twenty-five years old. Once he made that decision, his life got simpler. Why simpler and not harder? Now, his thoughts were more focused on this singular goal. His "certainty of intent" required him to ask some important questions to help him achieve this goal. Who are his climbing partners? How much money does he have to raise? What route is he going to take? Where are the base camps located, and how long will he be at each one? What kind of equipment does he have to take?

Most people would think that this one decision made Jamie's life infinitely more difficult, but in fact, his life became pretty simple. Not easy, but simple. He had a goal and began to execute against it. This vision now directed his life's steps. And the ultimate outcome, then, was that he climbed Mount Everest—not once, but multiple times.

Certainty of intent is designed and created to reinforce the vision through intentional execution. Actions are focused clearly on the vision.

From Photographs to Manufacturing: The Story of Eric Naaman

Eric was a very successful photographer and he seemed content in his career, but as he created time and space to think about his long-term future in a challenged industry, he knew he had come to a fork in the road and wanted to do something different. In seeking his clarity of vision, Eric knew he wanted a specific kind of company, based on his previous experience, so he established four criteria by which to conduct his search for the acquisition of a business: A cashflow positive company, a good product that he could stand behind, an ability to generate revenue when he was not present, and finally, a company where he could add value quickly due to a previously poor marketing effort. After a three-year search effort, Eric and his friend Robert Brooker landed on a company in the manufacturing industry.

He and his business partner bought a small, $4 million-in-revenue steel manufacturing company, Damotech, in Montreal, Canada, in 2010. Eric and Robert agreed to be co-CEOs, although it was something Eric had never done before. He'd been an individual business owner for years. He was really an artist and an entrepreneur more than anything else, and now he was becoming the co-CEO of a small manufacturing company. By necessity Eric started to learn how to be a CEO. That meant learning finance, marketing to a new industry, products, systems, processes, people, culture, and, in short, how to build a successful business.

On the personal side, at the time I started mentoring him in 2015, he had just stopped dating a young woman in Montreal. And as he talked to me about her, I could tell he still had a deep affection for her. I asked him why he had stopped dating her and he said, "Well, it just didn't seem like it was going to work."

I said, "Well, the first thing I want you to do is call her back and tell her how you feel." And he agreed. He called Cleo and told her how he felt. She shared with him how she felt, and they began dating again. They are now five years into their relationship, and it is very special and positive.

As he was building his manufacturing company, he ran into all the issues and struggles of being the CEO of a small business in a new industry and looked for ways to overcome them. Eric applied the principles of clarity of vision and certainty of intent in a very deliberate way to each of the four buckets of his life: family, business, community, and self. And today he is running a very profitable, $25-million-in-revenue manufacturing company, which he fully acquired in 2017, growing at over 30 percent per year. Additionally, he has a great family life, he is committed to serving his community, and his personal life is very fulfilling.

He's become an extraordinary CEO. He has built a remarkable business culture. He asks all the right questions, he makes decisions predicated on the right principles, and he believes in building teams by inspiring self-achievement through an exceptional work experience. In fact, one of his employees talked to the *Montreal Gazette*, Quebec's leading English newspaper, about this great boss for whom he was working. Following diligence by the paper, a front-page story was written featuring Eric in an article titled, "His Name Is Eric Naaman. You Might Call Him the Dream Boss."

He has clarity of vision, certainty of intent, and the power of values. Those three principles, when applied with others shared in this book, have helped make him the remarkably successful person he is today.

As an entrepreneur, I have always had the desire to live a purposeful life. What Warren shares in these pages is a methodology to develop a higher level of introspection, to commit to making conscious decisions, and to influence outcomes. Being able to have clarity of vision in all spheres of one's life, to act with intent and to respect one's values in the process, is a delicate balancing act that Warren has mastered. By applying the principles in this book, you will see that opportunities that present themselves start to collide with goals that you had set for yourself, propelling you to a higher level of achievement, to living a life by design. This approach has had an immeasurable influence over every facet of my life and, coming from someone as accomplished as Warren, is all the more compelling. He is living proof that doing well and doing good are not mutually exclusive.

—Eric Naaman, CEO, Damotech and Entrepreneur

My Journey to the White House

Sometime in late 1972, at the age of twenty-nine, I was having lunch with some friends and one of them, a retired four-star general, asked me if I'd ever heard of the White House Fellows program. I said I had not. He said he would send an application to me and that it was something for which I should apply. I received the extensive application, took a look at it, and put it in my desk drawer. At the time I was CEO of a small financial services company and had three young children.

A few months later, I was cleaning out my desk because I was moving to a new office, and in so doing I came across the application. I was intrigued, and I wanted to know how I would compare with other people around the country who might also apply. So, I filled it out and put it in the mail, never expecting to hear anything else.

The White House Fellows program was designed by John Gardner, the secretary of health and human services, and Lyndon Johnson, the president of the United States. The purpose was to bring to Washington, DC, successful people early in their career who could benefit from learning in close proximity to the key decision makers in government, and then return to their communities and use that knowledge to benefit their own communities. It was not an internship; you were selected on the basis of being able to make an immediate impact and be a regular member of the staff.

Having sent it off, I didn't expect to hear anything back, and I continued on with my life. About three months later, I received a letter indicating that I was one of about a hundred national semifinalists, and I could choose one of ten interviewing centers around the United States, where I would go and meet with members of the Commission on White House Fellows. (Much later I found out that there were several thousand applicants that year.) The purpose of the commission was to interview each person over several days and ascertain who would be their first recommended national finalist and who would be the alternate.

I chose Denver, Colorado. I was surprised by the quality of the people who were there—astronauts, authors, athletes, and scholars of all types. All were well-rounded and accomplished. It was a wonderful opportunity for me to meet some great people, one of whom was Roger Porter, a Harvard professor. We became great friends.

At the end of three days of scheduled interviews, they brought us together to announce that I was the first choice and another person was the alternate. I became a national finalist for a White House Fellowship.

Roger Porter was in that same competition and was not chosen, but he and I stayed in contact, and I continued to encourage him to apply the following year to see if he would be selected. Indeed, he was selected that next year, and we hired him on our White House staff after his selection. He arrived in DC just two days prior to the vice president becoming president.

Once the national finalists had been chosen, we went to Airlie House, a diplomatic retreat in Virginia. There were some thirty-seven national finalists, all of whom were just really terrific. I was honored to be in their company and knew there was no chance that I would be selected.

Before we arrived, the FBI conducted a full field investigation on us, which consisted of about a hundred pages of information starting from the time we entered school to the current time. We also went through many rounds of interviews. At the end of that week, I was honored to be one of seventeen who were selected as White House Fellows, and the first in history from Arizona. The other fellows who had been selected were just outstanding and, as I discovered over time, each was a remarkable person who contributed significantly to the government during their fellowship year. All have gone on to have exceptional careers in a variety of fields. I was privileged to associate with them for my fellowship year and have continued to be so through our annual reunions in the years since. Subsequently, I was able to give back to the program by being selected to be a member of the Commission on White House Fellows.

We then had to interview with our potential principal, which could be the president, the vice president, or a cabinet secretary. I was ultimately selected by the secretary of commerce, Fred Dent, to serve as his special assistant. In the fall of 1973, I was asked by Secretary Dent to be one of two people from Commerce to lead the first-ever executive-level trade mission in the history of the United States to the Soviet Union. The official delegation leader was a man named Tony Turner, who was the assistant secretary of commerce.

We traveled to the Soviet Union with a representative group of CEOs who were from big companies—PepsiCo, John Deere, IBM, Macrodata, Baldwin Tires, and so forth. We assisted them in negotiating trade agreements while in the Soviet Union.

Before departing for Russia, we developed a clear vision of the outcomes we desired. We then acted intentionally to achieve those stated outcomes and were successful in our efforts. Upon coming home from the trade mission, we learned that Richard Nixon had named his choice to be vice president following the resignation of Spiro Agnew. His choice was Gerald Ford, the House minority leader.

Through a good friend, Richard Eyre, I was introduced to Tom Hart, who was serving as the interim appointments secretary to President Richard Nixon. Tom felt I should get to know Vice President Ford, so Tom made an introduction to his chief of staff. I subsequently was asked to join the staff of the vice president, which turned out to be fortuitous.

I worked on his staff as a special assistant for scheduling. I was there the last several months of Richard Nixon's administration, during the Watergate scandal. It was a pivotal time in American history. To watch the peaceful transfer of power through a constitutional process was an incredible experience. To be able to have real-time conversations with all the key principals who were involved in that historic time was, perhaps, the greatest learning experience of my life.

It was also a wonderful time for our family. We had three children when we arrived in DC, and our fourth was born there. Our young family was right in the middle of American history, and we took full advantage of it. We visited every museum, historical site, and monument in Northern Virginia. Washington is alive with ideas, so whether at dinner parties or more informal gatherings, there were always discussions about ideas, politics, and personalities. Our children, though young, had amazing experiences and adventures. Our oldest son, Eric, remembers that time fondly. As I would, on occasion, have to go into work on Saturday, I would take Eric with me. He has great memories of playing football with the president in the hallway just outside the Oval Office. It was a very special time for our family.

The adrenaline would be flowing every day when I made my commute from McLean, Virginia, to DC, down the George Washington Memorial Parkway on my twenty-minute drive to enter the gates of the White House compound. The work environment was so stimulating and challenging. Every day was a different set of issues and personalities. My job was to facilitate, balance, and schedule all of the people who wanted to see the president. I prepared all of the president's schedules, but he, ultimately, signed off on all agenda items himself. There was both the public side of the presidency and the private one. My focus was all the public activities and private meetings for the president. I was part of the advance team that traveled to all the international locations where the president would be meeting with foreign heads of state to plan the details of the trip, meetings, and events. I had to interact with the vice president, chief of staff, cabinet secretaries, the First Lady, and the White House senior staff. I found them all to be intelligent, dedicated, reasoned, political, and committed to the president's agenda. There were, of course, personal agendas as well; however, generally, as a group, the senior team played well together.

The president was hosting the king of Norway, King Olaf. People looked around the White House and determined that I was the highest ranking Norwegian on the staff. I was invited to a small, intimate dinner with about twenty people. I was seated next to Dr. Henry Kissinger, secretary of state, who was seated next to the king. I was able to dazzle the secretary and the king with my limited vocabulary of Norwegian words. A good night for all.

State dinners, press conferences, Air Force One, heads of state, cabinet meetings, senior staff meetings, and representing the president of the United States were all heady things for a thirty-one-year-old farm kid from Minnesota. I learned a lot, made mistakes, learned again, and tried to do my best to serve—a distinct privilege indeed.

> We gained a great appreciation for American history, politics, institutions, and ideas. Going to work at the White House every day was exhilarating and exciting.

We gained a great appreciation for American history, politics, institutions, and ideas. Going to work at the White House every day was exhilarating and exciting. We were fortunate to have had this time in our lives. We gained friends and learned lessons that have lasted our entire lives.

During that time I was able to observe and participate, along with all the principals who were involved in that entire process, in the elevation of the man for whom I was working to the presidency. On

August 9, 1974, I led Gerald Ford into the East Room of the White House, where he was sworn in as president of the United States.

The people that President Ford appointed to special positions in his administration demonstrated to me the very principles we are discussing. He was thoughtful and intentional about his decisions and appointments, using strategic initiatives to accomplish the desired outcomes. Intentionality leads to success for the task at hand. That success may lead to unforeseen opportunities that can change our lives, as it did his. I saw these ideas in play and being executed every day in and around the White House. The people with whom I interacted served our country in notable ways during, and for decades following, the Ford presidency. Among them were: Nelson Rockefeller, Don Rumsfeld, Dick Cheney, Jack Marsh, Bob Gates, Brent Scowcroft, Colin Powell, Bill Seidman, Henry Kissinger, Ann Armstrong, and George H. W. Bush. Among the many outstanding people with whom I worked during the Ford administration, there are three who stand out as good examples of the three principles of leadership which we discussed earlier. First was Bob Gates, who best exemplified clarity of vision. We were the same age; he was working for General Brent Scowcroft, director of the National Security Council, a great man, and so we had a lot of interaction. To me, Bob always seemed to have a long-term view of issues and events affecting the world and the United States specifically. He always operated with the utmost integrity and thoughtfulness. I saw this later as he was named director of the CIA, president of Texas A&M University, and secretary of defense. During our nearly fifty years of friendship, he has been unwavering in his vision of, and commitment to, the United States and its best interests.

General Colin Powell best typified the principle of certainty of intent. He had exceptional social interaction skills, which enabled him to gain people's trust quickly. This allowed him to engage them in a common cause of intentional execution on almost any issue. He was a White House Fellow the year before me, and so we interacted within that circle. I got to know him as a young army major and watched his growth and contribution to government over four decades. As chairman of the joint chiefs of staff and secretary of state, he would host our public policy conference at the Defense and State Departments. His intentionality in his career, as the leader during Desert Storm and in his time as secretary of state, defines him well for me.

Finally, the man who best defined the power of values was George H. W. Bush. His energy and enthusiasm were present in all that he did. I never saw him deviate from his core beliefs and values. First among them was his love and commitment to his family. He and Barbara were so fond and proud of their children at all times. His family was the bedrock of all that he did. His dedication to and belief in America and what it stood for were so fundamental to him. He probably had the best resume of any person who became president. I first associated with him when he was chairman of the Republican National Committee, ambassador to China, and director of the CIA. I interacted with him when he was vice president and again when he was president. In every circumstance he was completely consistent in honoring and living his values. He served as a great example to me.

Intentionality Matters

Intentionality matters in everything; it qualifies every activity. We should be cautious about getting caught up in unintentional acts, though sometimes there are issues beyond our control.

Intentionality and success are closely linked. What we do on a daily and weekly basis demonstrates our intent. Executing our intent makes us more efficient, effective, and productive.

Part of intentionality is the ability to specifically define what it is we are going to do every day and have that list of actions be what drives us. Part of committing to a higher level of discipline is moving into a discussion of time management. All of us have the opportunity to be frivolous with our time. The amount of time we waste is extraordinary—perhaps even more so today, given the advance of technology and its availability.

When I'm mentoring a CEO, the first thing we do is have the CEO write down everything they are doing in a time log. Then we take that time log and divide it into four categories, those four buckets we listed earlier: family, business, community, and self. Almost everything we do fits into one of those buckets. We then break down the buckets into the hours and percentage of time spent on all activities/ tasks during their days and weeks.

When I analyze the time logs, it shows me everything they've done and all the areas of good and bad time management. I can take almost anyone's time log and give them back a significant percent of their time because of how frivolous most people are with time. If you can create a more efficient use of your time, you can be much more effective.

If the average person today lives to be about eighty years of age, calculate your age as a percentage of eighty, and the balance is the percentage of your life you have left to create the life you want to live. Of the majority of people with whom I have spoken, more than half of their life is behind them. So the question is, are they happy? Are their lives exactly what they want them to be?

What is the balance of our life going to be? How do we create the life we really want to live, or how do we make modifications to make our current life even better? Can we lead a life by design?

You can make significant changes in your levels of success and happiness when you embrace a life that aligns with your certainty of intent. As you'll see in the next two stories, the transformation can be nothing short of amazing.

Massey Ferguson Case Study: Certainty of Intent

My wife, Carson, and I were visiting Hong Kong, attending a YPO University event in 1992. While there I met a man named Victor Rice.

Until a few days prior to his trip to Hong Kong, Victor had been the CFO of a 150-year-old Canadian company called Massey Ferguson, which produced farm machinery. Just a few days before his arrival in Hong Kong, he had become the CEO of the company. It was a company that, while old and strong in its industry, was losing money and having a very difficult time.

As we spoke, he told me about his transition from CFO to CEO, and we talked about the challenges and difficulty of the business and what he was going back to face after Hong Kong. Over the next several hours, we shared ideas about how to turn around companies; how to think about them differently; how to act on them differently; what roles clarity of vision, certainty of intent, and the power of values play in such turnarounds; and how he might use those to his advantage.

About a week after I returned home from that trip, Victor called me and asked if I would join the board of directors of Massey Ferguson. I said I didn't typically join companies that seemed to be on the verge of bankruptcy, but he asked if I would come to Toronto and share my thoughts with the board of directors, which I agreed to do.

I flew to Toronto for the board meeting, and we had a robust discussion around ideas that we could use to turn the company around. Of the seven members on the board, there were three who were particularly negative and didn't feel like it was possible to turn the company around and felt that bankruptcy was the only option. In fact, those three board members resigned shortly thereafter. However, Victor was very positive and believed it could be turned around. He believed he could put together a management team that could do just that.

Doing this would involve the cooperation of the Canadian government. It would be hard for them to help us, but we were talking about twenty-five thousand Canadian jobs. The government agreed.

Victor and his management team did an exceptional job. We added some strong board members, including Bob Gates, a former director of the CIA and old friend from Washington, DC. We continued to work hard as a board and support Victor and his management team. And in just a couple of years, they had turned the company around; it was profitable.

We then moved the company to Buffalo, New York, so we could have a wider diversification of shareholders. We renamed the company Varity, then subsequently acquired a company in the United Kingdom by the name of Lucas, so the company became LucasVarity. We forged ahead by merging these two companies, moving the headquarters to London, and then ultimately selling the company for multiple billions of dollars to an American company. For comparison purposes, at the time I joined Massey Ferguson's board of directors, it was about a $3 billion company, and at the time we sold it, it was about a $9 billion company.

Again, it's about having clarity of vision and certainty of intent, then powering the culture with strongly shared values based on performance. This must be driven and led by the CEO, and in this case Victor Rice and his COO, Tony Andrews, were exceptional in every way.

Rise from the Ashes:
The Story of Marc Rousso

Another made-for-TV turnaround story started with the financial crisis of 2008. At the time of the financial crisis, Marc Rousso, CEO of JayMarc Homes, was an established land developer in the greater Seattle area. The recession decimated his company. He and his partner, Jay Mezistrano, lost everything—and I mean *everything*. Casualties of the recession for Marc and Jay were the loss of their company, employees, rental houses, essentially all assets. The recession also left them with $2.5 million in debt. To make matters worse, Marc needed to have brain surgery, from which he successfully recovered.

We had a chance meeting in Miami, after his brain surgery, and began to discuss some of the principles I often spoke about. He was very emotional in discussing the magnitude of his loss. I learned he had not only lost his business but also his confidence.

During that time he was also experiencing stress in his marriage and family life, as one can imagine with two toddlers under the age of two. So, the difficulty of what he was going through was multiplied several times over.

I said, "Well, Marc, what do you want to do?"

Marc said, "I'd like to be an amazing husband and father and build a respected custom home building company in the Seattle marketplace." He had clarity of vision.

Next, we spent time on his certainty of intent. How would he execute the very principles we had been discussing? He accepted coaching and new ideas. He applied them conscientiously to all he was doing.

He rebuilt his company with a great corporate culture—using collaboration, consensus, transparency, and vulnerability. He's helped his employees make changes through his own coaching and teaching. He carefully hired his staff and curated learning content, which helped them to grow their own leadership and knowledge.

At the time of the recession he had about a $50 million-in-revenue business. Today he has a $70 million-in-revenue business. He's one of the largest and most respected spec/custom home builders in his market, having won many local and national awards for service, design, operational excellence, and company culture.

Most importantly, he paid attention to his marriage and family, and they are as happy as they've been in many years. He started going on one-on-one daddy/son-daughter trips each year, from a family perspective. Marc made the relationship with his wife, Leslie, a priority, going on regular date nights and multiple couple trips throughout the year. He has been challenging himself physically and personally, completing a half-Ironman and taking up tennis after a thirty-year absence. Something superexciting for Marc was reenergizing his DJ career after a twenty-five-year absence; he already has a number-one song on the charts and a goal of DJing at clubs, festivals and parties.

> No matter your circumstances or age, when you decide to take your life to the next level and have clarity of vision and certainty of intent, there is truly no limit to what you can accomplish.

You see, everything is possible. I have watched Marc grow personally and professionally, but what I'm most proud of is seeing his confidence and leadership blossom. No matter your circumstances or age, when you decide to take your life to the next level and have clarity of vision and certainty of intent, there is truly no limit to what you can accomplish.

I consider Warren Rustand to be a second father to me who has provided invaluable guidance on leadership, excellence, family values, purpose, goals, and vision. Rarely do you come across a man that loves you unconditionally, inspires you to be your best self, and teaches you to live a life you've always dreamed of having. There is no better resource to take you to the next level than Warren.

—Marc Rousso, CEO of JayMarc Homes

CHAPTER 4

PRINCIPLE OF LEADERSHIP NUMBER THREE: THE POWER OF VALUES

What you have does not determine who you are.
Who you are determines what you have.

—George Gan

We influence others by how we live our lives, the example we set, and the modeling we do. This third principle of leadership, *the power of values*, is about the journey once we say, "Okay, if this is where I'm going (vision), and this is what I'm going to do (intent), then what values will guide me on my journey?"

Our values are the boundaries or guardrails of our journey. These are the behaviors and actions that others see in us. When Gerald Ford was transitioning from the vice presidency to the presidency, he chose Don Rumsfeld to lead the transition, and, ultimately, become chief of staff.

One day, just prior to the swearing in of the new president, Rumsfeld asked me what I thought was a simple question: "For whom do you work?"

I thought, quite smugly, that I knew the answer. I said, "I work for my country, my president, and my chief of staff."

He said, "You have those answers in exactly the wrong order." Rumsfeld said that the president would take care of the country, that he would take care of the president, and that I reported to him. What he was really saying, I believe, was that he valued loyalty a great deal and I should be aware of that.

The Power of Values

When determining our personal values, the first thing to do is to decide who we are at our core. Stephen Covey, in his book *The 7 Habits of Highly Successful People*, said there are three moments of truth in a human's life: "The first is when we discover our core beliefs and values. The second is when we commit to our core beliefs and values. And the third is when we act on our core beliefs and values."[2]

I embrace Covey's views. I think it often takes some people a long time to determine who they are at their core. Once they define, commit to, and act on that knowledge, they can model their behavior for others. Anyone who watches them can then understand who they are. Core beliefs and values give consistency and predictability to one's life, which are necessary to achieve the outcomes that you desire.

My vision was to play basketball at a high level, so at the age of sixteen, I made some fundamental choices about my behavior and my health. I decided I would never drink alcohol, use drugs, use tobacco products, or drink coffee. And now, in my more mature years, I have *still* never done those things.

So, am I healthier? Yes, I think so. Probably healthier than most people my age. I'm still competing athletically and doing a wide range

---

2   Stephen Covey, *The 7 Habits of Highly Effective People*, 30th Anniversary Ed. (New York: Simon and Schuster, 2020).

of physical activities. One of my values is good health and enjoying a healthy lifestyle.

I think we have to know our core beliefs and values, and then make choices based on those values. Our values can morph and change over time through circumstances, experiences, and learning. As leaders in our families, businesses, and communities, we should appreciate the signals we send by our behavior and actions. Many people watch us and, for good or bad, we give others a great deal of information about ourselves by how we behave and reflect our values.

Selecting Family Values

As a family we initiated a process for selecting our values, and you can do the same.

1. Have several three-by-five cards in front of each member of the family.

2. Ask them to write a word on each card that represents a value.

3. Then through group discussion eliminate words that are the same or very similar and choose only one of the words for each similar meaning.

4. Then narrow the total number to under ten.

5. Discuss with your family the meaning of each word until you have agreement on the definitions.

6. Select words that are unique to your family.

7. Talk about the definitions until there is agreement for each word.

8. Then ask each member of the family if they agree with and will live the values chosen.

9. Finally choose the final group of words and the descriptive sentence that goes with each word.

10. Invite the family to commit to behavior that is consistent with those values.

11. The final step is to memorialize the values in a special way and place them in your home where all can see them.

Our family values are the following:

Listen

Dream wildly

Be humble

Give back

Cherish family

Send out love

Be positive

Laugh at yourself

Forgive

Our family values list is on a metal strip between our utility room and our kitchen, where there is a lot of foot traffic. Our vision statement, which I'll discuss in Chapter 6, is near our front door and can be seen easily as you enter our home. By reading those two statements—our values list and our vision statement—you will know a great deal about our family.

We try diligently to live our values every day. Our children and grandchildren know that if we violate our values, we will have a discussion about it. We all strive to live our lives consistent with the vision and values that we have for our family. Our vision and values become a very important part of the way in which we live our lives and serve as guides for all of our decision-making. They govern our thoughts, actions, and interactions. We are blessed to have a wonderful family. We have seven children, Eric, William, Scott, Kenady, Brett, Garrett, and Clark, all of whom make me proud to be their father every day. They live these values and serve as a great example for me of how to live their beliefs and values. Each has excelled based on their potential and vision for their lives. We are immensely proud of each of them.

It's just as important that we find friends who align with our own values and perspective. In this way, we are constantly mirroring the behavior we wish to see in ourselves.

Providence Service Corporation Case Study: The Trifecta of Principles

The story of Providence Service Corporation is an example of all three of the principles—clarity of vision, certainty of intent, power of values.

I served as the lead outside director for Providence Service Corporation for several years. A private equity company bought a significant stake in the company, and a member of that firm joined the board of directors. Due to the underperformance of the company, a decision by the board was made to terminate the CEO and CFO and take the business in another direction.

As a lead director, I needed to do the terminations, which I did, though it was very difficult because both men were good friends. The end result was that the board asked me if I would become the CEO, and I said I would for a period of three years only.

Shortly after becoming CEO, I went to the analysts on Wall Street and said, "There are five things that we're going to do to grow the company, and you can measure our performance on how we do on these five things."

The first was to operate the company more efficiently and effectively. The second was to grow organically at least 10 percent per year. The third was to become acquisitive, to look for major acquisitions. The fourth was to invest in technology, to be a technology leader. And the fifth was to build a high-performance, incentive-based culture for all employees.

We began to work on these goals, and every quarter we reported on our progress. Within six months we had essentially doubled the share price.

When I became CEO, the numbers were an eleven-dollar share price, EBITDA (earnings before interest, tax, depreciation and amortization—a measure of a company's operating performance) of $60 million, ten thousand employees, and $985 million in revenue. Fast-forward thirty months—the share price was north of fifty dollars a share, we had seventeen thousand employees and $2.1 billion in revenue, and the EBITDA was about $120 million a year.

This was all done by having a very clear vision. Then we acted with intentionality on that vision every day, and we built a strong values-based culture that respected and valued individual employees.

We inherited a service-based company with some significant challenges, including pay discrimination, gender discrimination, and even racial discrimination in some cases. It was a very difficult time. Thanks to an extraordinary HR leader, Justina Sanchez-Cox, we were able to resolve most of these issues for our employees, which enabled us to develop a very strong culture.

Once the employees felt valued, they coalesced around the notion of who they were, the service they were providing, the gift they were giving, and the way in which they could make the company more successful. Therefore, the business did very, very well.

What Does It Look Like to Commit?

Since our vision, intent, and values drive our decision-making, we should strive for consistency across all facets of our lives.

Among the very finest people we know are those who are completely consistent across all dimensions of their lives. They're enjoyable to be around because we always know what they're about. They're more easily definable.

There are great examples of leaders, historically and currently, whose lives have reflected the consistency of their vision, intent, and values. We may think of Mahatma Gandhi, Nelson Mandela, Winston Churchill, Mother Teresa, Margaret Thatcher, Ronald Reagan, Bill Gates, and Warren Buffett. These are people who consistently acted on their established core belief system, both in their public and private lives. This is not to say they lived perfectly. It is to say that their lives reflected their value system, which in turn affected the lives of others.

An interesting case in point is Gandhi. After the Great Salt March covering some 250 miles, with thousands of followers, he was invited to speak to Parliament in the United Kingdom. He spoke for a very long time without interruption, and without notes of any kind. When he finished, one of the questions the media asked was "Mr. Gandhi, how can you speak so eloquently and so articulately for so long without notes of any kind?"

He said, "What I say is what I believe, and what I believe is what I do." His words, beliefs, and actions were completely aligned. His values were consistently aligned with his thoughts and his actions.

Another great leader who was completely committed to his vision was Nelson Mandela, who spent twenty-one years as a prisoner on Robyn's Island near Cape Town and six more years at Pollsmoor Prison in Cape Town. During his incarceration he began his transformation from prisoner to president.

I had a chance to meet him in the early nineties in Washington, DC. I spent only a short time with him, but he was exactly the person I thought he was going to be. I also met his personal secretary who served him the last nineteen years of his life, a woman named Zelda. She described Mandela exactly as I experienced him when I met him. There was no inconsistency. Every little thing she described about him reinforced all of the values and qualities that I observed. Through his struggles, he came to a greater understanding of his personal account-ability for his vision, intent, and values. He lived what he believed every day.

I have the opportunity to see and be with many CEOs, entre-preneurs, and other leaders in my global travels. All have unique and interesting personalities and backgrounds. It's always interesting to meet those who are completely aligned in their belief system. Those who are the same onstage and offstage. The goal is to become so con-sistent with our own values that there's never a question about who we are and for what we stand.

A Life-Changing Decision: The Story of Pat Manley

Our lives move on our own momentum sometimes due to chance, serendipity, or personal choice. For some there comes an opportunity or desire to alter their life, through choice or intervention. Sometimes that change can be subtle and nuanced, and sometimes it's dramatic.

My friend Pat Manley played football at the University of Arizona. Shortly after graduation he joined the pro rodeo circuit. Fighting through multiple injuries and pain, he developed an addiction to drugs and then alcohol. He was soon dependent on both. He was trapped in that lifestyle for many years. During this time his wife left him, leaving their son in Pat's care. He loved and cared for his son, who has grown to be an outstanding young man.

One late afternoon, drained of all energy and hope, he sat on a street corner in Tucson, Arizona, not knowing what to do and uncertain of what the future would be. But he did know that he had to go home and put his son to bed. He put his son to bed, and then he did an interesting thing, something he hadn't done in many years. He prayed.

Pat had spent a year studying the priesthood early in his life, prior to entering the University of Arizona. He had never forgotten his faith or values from his youth. Just before he was going to carry out his plan, he knelt down at the end of his son's bed, and he said one simple phrase: "Lord, please take this malady from me." He stood up, and from that moment, never had another desire to consume drugs or alcohol.

Thirty years later, he's still alive and living his life in service to others. He built the Hedrick House, which is a place for people to dry out and begin to turn their lives around. He also bought a closed school, converted it, and between the two facilities he has a hundred beds available for people who want to try to change their life from alcohol and drugs to something else, something better. I greatly admire Pat and the impact he has had on the lives of others.

Whether change comes in an instant or it's a pattern of struggling, falling back, and getting up, keep marching toward that distant landmark, your landmark. Sooner or later, it won't be so distant.

I have known Warren Rustand since 1966; he had just finished his basketball career with University of Arizona and the Golden State Warriors. He was my brother's basketball coach for the basketball team at the University of Arizona. His wife was classmates with my sister at West Phoenix High School. Since I first met him, our paths have crossed a number of times, including in business, religion, and many, many personal interactions. I have known him to be an upstanding, honest, and trustworthy human being. His involvement with community, family, and church leave not much to be desired. I value his friendship and guidance and hope to be associated with him for the rest of the game.

—Pat Manley, Founder / Owner, Johnson
Manley Lumber Company

Achieving Authenticity

Authenticity is oftentimes difficult for people to achieve, particularly in a world of social media. It's really important, however, because with authenticity often come vulnerability and transparency.

When I was thirty years old, I had an experience with President Gerald Ford that illustrates my beliefs about authenticity. About thirty days into his presidency, it became obvious to me that I wasn't competent enough to be there.

I had gotten my position at the White House because of a nationally competitive process called the White House Fellows program. And the more we got into Ford's presidency, the more I realized his team was more experienced, more political, and more knowledgeable than I.

I was interacting with Bob Gates, Jack Marsh, Henry Kissinger,

Brent Scowcroft, Don Rumsfeld, Dick Cheney, and other outstanding people in his administration, members of our senior team. And here I was, the odd kid on the block, rubbing shoulders with world leaders and feeling totally out of my league. Yes, I worked in the White House, but I was still the farm kid from Minnesota.

Because I influenced the president's schedule and all of his daily activities, I was just sure I was going to make a mistake and embarrass him publicly.

I knew I had to resign. That was the only option.

One morning we had a short meeting in the Oval Office. Everyone drifted out after the meeting, but I hung around to see if I could talk to the president for a few minutes. I was a bit nervous, but I wanted to express my shortcomings and leave the decision up to the president. I knew I would be okay with whatever he decided.

I said, "Mr. President, may I speak with you?"

And he said, "Sure. Please sit down."

I sat down and said, "Mr. President, I'm not smart enough. I don't have enough experience. I'm not political enough. I'm afraid I'm going to make a mistake in some way. I don't want to do anything that will harm you or your presidency. Therefore, here's my letter of resignation." And I placed my brief letter on his desk.

President Ford looked at it for a short time, then he turned his chair and looked out across the south lawn of the White House and toward the rose garden. He sat with his back to me for what seemed to be eight hours, although it was probably about ten seconds. I was anxiously waiting for his answer.

Finally, he turned around and said, "Warren, the very fact that you've told me this qualifies you to be here." I was surprised. But I came to understand that because I was vulnerable, transparent, and honest, he knew he could trust me. And from that point on, he trusted me with issues and information that no thirty-year-old farm kid without experience should have ever been entrusted to have. We developed a good working relationship. The time I spent in the White House would influence virtually everything I did for the balance of my life.

Being vulnerable, authentic, and transparent does take focus. And there have been times in my life where I've struggled with it. I've had to battle with pride and ego, just as most of us do.

Any time life or our decisions throw us off our chosen path, remember those three great moments of truth:

Determine our core beliefs and values.

Commit to those core beliefs and values.

Act on those core beliefs and values.

PART II

FIVE PRINCIPLES OF PERSONAL GREATNESS

Perform your best when it matters most.

Everything I have learned, and teach, mentor, or speak about, is based on my personal life experiences. I have spoken about the **Five Principles of Personal Greatness** for forty years.

Everything I have learned or teach about I have applied to the multiple companies where I have been the CEO, and to the not-for-profits and boards on which I sit. Some were large companies, some small companies. Lest you think I'm perfect, you should know I also have both business and personal failures in my background. Sometimes it was because I didn't always adhere to my principles. I lost my focus.

The **Five Principles of Personal Greatness** might, on the surface, seem similar to the **Three Principles of Leadership** in Part I, but there is a distinct difference—the first three are philosophic and directional, and these other five are the specific application of the first three.

The Five Principles Work

Each one of these principles starts with an action verb. These are not passive concepts. When I teach these principles in person, at events, as a CEO, or in one-on-one mentoring, I take people through a methodology, and I can say to them, "If you practice these principles I am going to share with you, they will change your life forever." I have watched people apply these concepts and observed what they can do for individuals. We've heard thousands of stories of leaders who have struggled and fought back when they became practitioners of these principles.

I have lived these principles virtually my entire life, and they have helped me move from an isolated farm in Minnesota to living a life by design, desire, and determination.

If you do the work and make the changes in your life to implement these principles and strategies, there's simply no end to the success you can achieve, and, importantly, you will feel much better about yourself.

Mindset Is Everything

For us to change our current state, we must change our mind. We must alter our way of thinking. Even when our body is fatigued, if our mind says, "Go a little further. Do a little more. Push a little harder," our body will listen. The body will follow the mind, so put your mind in the right place and you have the opportunity to be more successful. This applies to all areas of life, whether at home, in the boardroom, or in the locker room.

I've never been in a locker room with a group of basketball players prior to a game where we sat around talking about how bad we were. Have you? Can you imagine how defeated everyone would look and feel if the players were talking down their own abilities? "We're going to get killed today. This isn't going to work. We're not good enough. This is stupid. Why are we playing?"

There wouldn't be a reason to step onto the court with a negative mindset.

Instead of talking about the negatives, think about the positives, and the negatives will be overcome. Be positive and optimistic because our mindset controls our thinking and behavior.

We don't focus on negative thoughts and outcomes when we're preparing for a special event. So why would we do that if we're preparing for our own life each day? There are times when we awake and feel unhappy, frustrated, inadequate, or challenged. This is not uncommon. The key is that we should not look to others to make us happy or change our disposition. For some, life is one excuse after another. It's never our fault. The reality is, *our life is our fault*, either for good or for bad. We are all self-made. We are accountable and responsible for our choices, decisions, and thoughts.

Some people are more naturally disciplined than others. Healthy habits and a disciplined mind can be learned at a very young age. But how difficult is it for someone in their thirties, forties, fifties, or sixties to adopt new habits? It has been said that it takes somewhere between twenty-one and sixty days to adopt a new habit. If we persist and are diligent about our discipline in developing a new habit, then each time we attempt to change, it becomes marginally easier. Each time we eliminate a bad habit and replace it with a good habit, we grow exponentially.

Just decide. Make the choice to be great.

I decided to play basketball at the highest level possible for me; therefore, I needed to create good habits and eliminate other habits that weren't as good for me if I was going to achieve my goal.

Replace old habits with new habits. We are what we think. And what we think is what we become. Our understanding and acknowledgment of mindset is better developed as we come to know Kirsten Dermer.

I met Kirsten Dermer about ten years ago, when she attended a public policy conference that I was chairing. Petite in frame but a giant in disciplined habits, she races dirt bikes, runs half-marathons, and power lifts, none of which you would guess by looking at her. Her personal discipline is legend. It carries over to her role as CEO of her two companies and her personal life. One company builds skate parks, and the other makes extraordinary donuts. She is a very successful CEO in a male-dominated industry, construction. She does this by being very smart, disciplined, and always upgrading her habits through intense learning. She consistently replaces old habits with new and better habits, patterns, and rituals. She is constantly improving herself and her leadership. I have the greatest respect and admiration for her and what she has accomplished.

Warren Rustand is one of the most accomplished and impressive people I know. But that's not what makes him a great human being. He could just focus on building his businesses and creating maximum financial success for himself. Instead, he chooses to give an unimaginable amount of his time to mentoring and guiding people. It is impossible to overstate Warren's impact on literally thousands of entrepreneurs worldwide, including me.

—**Kirsten Dermer, CEO, Spohn Ranch, Inc.**

Life is a mindset. As I mentioned previously, in his book, *If I Can, You Can*, Dr. David Zelman talks about the two types of discussions we have with ourselves. The first is the fixed mindset or discussion. It is about repetition, consistency, predictability, and sameness. The second mindset is growth. It is about risk, advancement, the new, and the different. One is about scarcity, and the other about abundance. When we choose greatness, often the choice is between good, better, and best—not good and bad.

> When we choose greatness, often the choice is between good, better, and best— not good and bad.

As we work our way through these **five principles of personal greatness**, remember that your mindset is what is going to enable you to stay the course and increase your chances of success. If you find yourself veering off course at any time, all you have to do is remind yourself that you are in charge of your mind, and your mind controls your world.

Get back on course and stick with it. Your new life is just around the corner.

CHAPTER 5

THE FIRST PRINCIPLE OF PERSONAL GREATNESS: COMMITTING TO A HIGHER LEVEL OF PERSONAL DISCIPLINE

All the leaders I know are highly disciplined. They all have a particular way of doing what they do. Their success and structure can be attributed to their discipline—their habits, patterns, and rituals.

A recent survey article, "14 Things Ridiculously Successful People Do Every Day,"[3] featured billionaires, Olympians, CEOs, and other extraordinary people. Every single one of them mentioned that they have a discipline or a pattern that they start with each day. They do things differently than others.

Most people get up, go to the bathroom, brush their teeth, walk the dog, reach for their cell phone, turn on the TV, grab the newspaper, and eat whatever food is easiest. That means most people are doing what's easiest, not necessarily what's best.

---

3   Travis Bradberry, "14 Things Ridiculously Successful People Do Every Day," May 11, 2017, Inc. https://www.inc.com/travis-bradberry/14-things-ridiculously-successful-people-do-every-day.html.

But extraordinary people have healthy and intentional daily rituals and patterns that affect them in a very positive way. They have committed to personal discipline.

When you correct your mind, everything else falls into place. We are the totality of what we think. Our thoughts are who we become. Remember, words are who we want to be; actions are who we are. People watch our behavior and decide who we are not by what we say but by what we do.

And when we begin our days with simple but profound choices that set the tone for us to achieve our goals, the rest of our day falls more easily into place.

1-10-10-10

I've been doing the same thirty-one-minute ritual for forty-five years. When I speak to audiences, I always ask them, "What do you do first thing in the morning? What are your morning habits and patterns?"

The answers are predictable:

I get up.

I go to the bathroom.

I walk the dog.

I check my cell phone.

I make coffee.

I turn on the TV and watch the news.

I read the newspaper.

I fix breakfast.

After a minute of these standard answers, I say, "None of the things you suggested prepare you for success that day."

We know if we read a newspaper, most of it is negative, discouraging, heavily biased, or simply untrue. We know that if you reach for your cell phone to check email, messages, or news, much of it is negative. We know that if you turn on a TV, a great deal of it is negative or at the very least, a distraction and time waster. So, why would anybody do those things first thing in the morning? Most successful people don't have negative activities in the morning, but rather they concentrate on the positive.

The only way you're going to change your personal life, leadership, and potential greatness is to change your pattern. And you can do this in only thirty-one minutes a day.

The First Minute

The first thing I want you to do when you wake up in the morning is sit on the edge of your bed for one minute and ask yourself, "Why am I alive today? Why has my life been preserved for today? What is my purpose today?" It is the first thing on which we should focus. We know people who are driven by purpose are more successful than people who aren't. Therefore, the most important declaration we can make in the morning is to determine our purpose for the day.

Some days I have to be a tough negotiator or a compassionate team leader. Some days I have to be a patient teacher. Other days I need to be an engaged father. Every day I need to be an attentive husband. Some days I have multiple purposes over the course of the day, a combination of roles and goals. I may need to be a negotiator in the morning, but I've got to be a grandfather in the afternoon. Thinking about my primary purpose for one minute creates a laser-like focus on my highest priority or priorities for that day.

First Ten Minutes

Once you've determined what your daily purpose is, take ten minutes, find some nice and quiet place in your home, and reflect and be grateful for all you have. Speak it out loud, or quietly say it in your mind.

Be grateful for the sunrise, for another 86,400 seconds. Be grateful for your family. Be grateful for your business. Be grateful you live where you live—in your city, your community, in your great country. Be grateful because attitudes of gratitude put your mind in the place that allows you to be more successful.

Every morning in Arizona, I get to see the sunrise. Every evening I get to see the sunset. They are spectacular. In addition to that, I live in a great home. I have a wonderful family. I have a terrific business. I have a great life. I could fill up books with things for which to be grateful.

Having an attitude of gratitude is very important every morning. It could also be called meditation, but I call it gratefulness. Either way, take ten minutes to pause your life to give thanks. Here are some examples to get you started: "I am grateful for my family, sunrises and sunsets, our home, business colleagues, endless possibilities, great friends, new opportunities, my neighbors, community, and country. I am grateful for my freedoms, creativity, serving others, extended family, energy, fitness, and my commitment to being better and making the world better."

You can be thankful for anything that makes your day a little brighter! Making time and space to be grateful makes a difference.

Second Ten Minutes

For the second ten minutes, read something inspirational, something without any negative language or energy. I'm currently reading *The World's 100 Greatest Speeches,* which includes great speakers like Mandela, Reagan, Churchill, Gandhi, Kennedy, and Martin Luther King Jr. These inspiring messages lift my spirits and put me in a positive frame of mind. Other books—*Manual for Living* by Epictetus, *The Treasure Chest, Thank You, The Book of Positive Quotes,* and others—can help us be the better version of ourselves each day.

Third Ten Minutes

For the final ten minutes, write in your journal. Focus on the positive experiences of your life. Use those positive times to inspire and encourage those who will eventually read the journal. All of us have hard times, as well. Take from those times the lessons you have learned and how they can be applied to benefit the reader. Use the learning gained from adversity to help those who may need to hear of your experience and wisdom. My own view is that the details of the bad circumstances you had may not be as valuable as the great learning you have taken from it.

Additionally, your journal will become a part of your family genealogy and history. It will be read by scores of family members long after you are gone. Your legacy will be formed, to some degree, by what you write and the stories you tell. You can bring joy and happiness to countless others by the way in which you portray that which you have learned and experienced.

I have read the journals of many pioneers, leaders, and ordinary citizens, which are available to us. They amaze, enlighten, and illuminate the history, traditions, and way of life of those who have passed before us. Thanks to Reverend Peter Raible, I am reminded that:

We build on foundations we did not lay.

We warm ourselves by fires we did not light.

We sit in the shade of trees we did not plant.

We drink from wells we did not dig.

We profit from persons we did not know.

This is as it should be.

Together we are more than any one person could be.

Together we can build across the generations.

Together we can renew our hope and faith in the life that is yet to unfold.

Together we can heed the call to a ministry of care and justice.

We are ever bound in community.

May it always be so.

We stand on the shoulders of those who have gone before, and we learn from the contributions they have made.

Create Your Own Morning Routine

So how do you prepare for the day? You might have your own morning routine, and if it prepares you for the day and fills you with positivity, that's great! Some people don't integrate the 1-10-10-10 exactly as I do, but they substitute meditation or yoga. They're still doing the same kind of thought process; they're just using different vehicles for preparation. Allow your morning routine to create a foundation for the mind to lead you to success. Every day matters to the leader.

What you do first thing in the morning propels you to success. It is all about building yourself up for the challenge of the day. Every day is about advancing and getting better. Prepare yourself! In terms of those who prepare for each day, it is unbelievable how their family, business, community, and personal lives have changed. They see the world differently, more optimistically, more positively, and more enthusiastically. They have changed and so has the world in which they live.

Brian Brault, former global chair of EO and principal of PURE Wellness, has been practicing a morning routine for four years and contends that it has changed so much about his life. He is more optimistic, positive, and prepared for the day. He feels additional energy and focus for his activities.

Brian and I have the chance to teach and present together often. I am amazed at the precision he has in his preparation and the manner in which he presents his ideas. He is truly prepared for the day! What a great leader, friend, and influence for good.

The Body Follows the Mind

If you've done these exercises, you're thirty-one minutes into your day. You've defined your purpose, had ten minutes of gratefulness, ten minutes of reading positive things, and ten minutes of writing positive things. Where's your mind?

You're in a great position to have a great day! So, if you want to commit to personal discipline, the first piece of that is your mindset. You have to establish a mind that allows you to be more successful. The next piece is to create a body that will follow your mind, through daily exercise, healthy nutrition, and time management. You have built up your mind in positivity, and now you need to go release endorphins.

THE LEADER WITHIN US

Exercise

As soon as you've completed the thirty-one minutes, go do something physical. The body needs at least thirty minutes of rigorous exercise three to four times a week. Each of us should have 150 minutes of rigorous exercise every week. If we can do more, great.

Research suggests that exercise in the morning is more valuable than exercise in the evening or the afternoon. Why? Fatigue and focus over the course of the day can keep you from maximizing your workout performance. Seek to optimize your performance.

It's also important to go into each exercise period or each workout with specific goals in mind: *I want to burn seven hundred calories. I want to swim ten laps. I want to walk on the treadmill for thirty minutes.* Choose an exercise that works for you.

You should have cardio and weight training. Around your midthirties you begin losing lean muscle mass, and unless you're rebuilding that lean muscle mass, you will continue to lose it for the rest of your life. It doesn't regenerate unless you build it. So, you want to include some lifting—high reps, low weight—to build lean muscle mass. Also, some form of cardio workout is very important. This may include biking, rowing, running, swimming, and a variety of other related activities. It is important to raise your heart rate regularly. Choose the exercise pattern that is best for you and the activities in which you want to engage.

I certainly recognize that we have different stages and ages in life that make it more or less difficult to get our exercise on a regular basis. Young children usually get up early and want to snuggle or have special time with their parents. As our children grow into their teens and adulthood, we have more flexibility with our family and individual schedules. Each of us can determine a schedule that works best for us and our families as we pass through these various stages of life. The important thing is that it is a priority and that we are creative about how we achieve our goals. It is also possible to have other family members work out with us or be in the environment as we exercise, perhaps, modeling good practices and behavior.

One of the benefits of being in good physical and mental shape is the opportunity to say yes when our children ask us to do something that requires activity, effort, strength, or endurance. Being able to say yes to our children in this area of our lives often helps to build great parental relationships with them.

Time Management and Technology

The last piece to your morning routine is determining how you will manage your time so you can get more out of your day. And trust me, if you don't intentionally manage your time, it will manage you. You will recall that we discussed earlier in the book the fact that we have 86,400 seconds each day. About one third of that is spent sleeping, so the balance is ours to plan and manage. How well we do it will largely determine how effective we are at achieving our priorities.

One of the great challenges we all face is the use and management of our technology. Whether we are a migrant to or native of technology, we have been confronted with the amount of time we spend on our devices. Often our instincts to use the device run in conflict with other, often more important things we have to do. On a personal basis, we can do several things to practice better discipline.

Take a technology sabbatical for hours, days, or weeks. Turn off the device when you arrive home and concentrate on your primary relationships. Turn off your device two hours before you go to bed and don't turn it on until you are leaving for the office or your first activity of the day following your morning routine. Or keep the cell phone on silent so your core work is not interrupted, returning calls, texts, and emails at a later time.

In corporate America today, it's estimated that the average person spends a significant percent of their time, perhaps up to 20 percent, on their personal device during work hours. The cost to corporate America is truly significant—both in loss of productivity and in the knowledge that workers are being paid a portion of each day to post on social media, have personal phone calls, and respond to non-work-related texts and emails.

> Because my goal is to simplify life, I believe we have to create boundaries and reasonable expectations, whether they be for our work colleagues or our families.

Because my goal is to simplify life, I believe we have to create boundaries and reasonable expectations, whether they be for our work colleagues or our families. The reality is that most people rely on emails, texts, phone, and other messaging systems for work-related communication. But the sheer volume of communication can become overwhelming, especially if there isn't a system in place for processing that information.

I, like you, receive scores of emails, texts, and phone messages each day. It's not possible to respond to them all. If I tried, I would spend most of my day acting on the agenda of others rather than my own specific agenda. As soon as I react or respond to the messages coming in, I am working on that person's priorities and not my own.

I'm sure each of us has given some thought to how we communicate effectively, with the sheer number of contacts going up exponentially. I've developed a process that works for me and helps me manage my time so I can focus on my priorities. I check my email for thirty minutes in the morning. I check it again thirty minutes at midday, and I check it thirty minutes before I go home. I also have an outstanding colleague, Lysset Butler, who facilitates these activities and makes me much more efficient and effective. She's able to review and intervene in all forms of communication. She does this knowing what my priorities and her activities are, therefore allowing me to concentrate on what is most important for our family, business, and community.

People who know me well know that I won't respond to their texts or to an email right away unless it's urgent. I try to manage those expectations because reacting to other people's agendas has to come after my priorities and engagements, which are focused on moving toward my vision with certainty of intent.

It's important to have a distillation process that gets you down to the core number of items that truly need your attention. Without this process, you'll never get to your vision or intent.

Many people struggle in their lives because they can't figure out how to *elevate* what's most important, delay issues of lesser importance, and push aside the trivial.

Technology truly is wonderful. It's a great blessing, and a great curse. But without a process and focus on time management, we get sucked into the buzz of online news or social media platforms. It's a very short hop from checking your emails to watching some interesting YouTube videos to checking national news. And then you're down the rabbit hole. An hour later you snap out of it, only to realize you've spent too much time watching cute dog videos.

You might argue that cute dog videos are a far better use of time than scrolling through the national news, but remember, you're trying to create simplicity. The goal is to be intentional about your time and your life's goals.

This notion of certainty of intent is a powerful thing. It means waking up in the morning, sitting on the edge of your bed for a minute, and asking yourself, "Why am I alive today? What's my purpose for the day?" In my case, some days I have to be a great negotiator, some days a great father, some days a wonderful grandfather. Whatever I need to be that day, I want to be the best at it I can be. That requires me to be intentional with my time and my focus.

Change Your Mindset with a Morning Routine

In his book *Good to Great*, Jim Collins said, "Success is not a circumstance. It's a choice and discipline." You choose greatness. You decide to be great. Nobody's going to give it to you on a silver platter. Nobody's going to gift you with greatness.

If you're going to commit to discipline, then start by implementing a morning routine. If your mind is in the right place, everything else will work out. Never underestimate yourself. Life is nothing but a state of mind.

If you implement this morning routine and do it for sixty to ninety days, it will become a habit. And it will change your life, just like it's changed the lives of others in miraculous ways.

Jamie Douraghy wanted to win the gold medal and be the best fencer in the United States. He had to change his mindset at age fifty-two in order to reach his goal—and he did it. In fact, after winning three USA Fencing National Championships and having been on seven US teams for the World Fencing Championships, he's currently ranked second in the United States. In October of 2019, in Cairo, Jamie won the bronze medal in the world championships and led the US team to the silver medal, a US first. *And he's now sixty years old.* If he can reach his goals, there's no reason you can't reach yours.

A morning routine will lead to other healthier habits throughout the day. Small changes really do turn your life around. We gain more time and more confidence, and we become more optimistic about our lives and the many opportunities we will encounter.

Remember, we control all of these elements. We simply have to decide what we want to achieve. When we choose a higher level of personal discipline, we choose to live happier lives with greater purpose.

CHAPTER 6

THE SECOND PRINCIPLE OF PERSONAL GREATNESS: LIVING WITH PURPOSE—EVERY DAY

Don't worry about knowing. Prepare so you will be ready to know.

Mother Theresa said, "We can't all do great things, but we can all do little things with great love." Every large and small thing that we do we need to do with great purpose. And when we do that, we change outcomes.

Purpose takes us to a higher level. If we can discover our purpose each day, we inherently create an advantage for ourselves. Our purpose is what drives us. It is why we do what we do.

The ability to see each day and each activity within the context of purpose is very important. Purpose is the reason for which something is done. It is a person's sense of resolve or determination. Therefore, if we can live with purpose each day, it allows us to intently focus on our highest endeavor.

Kristina Scala taught me a great lesson about living with vision and purpose every day. She and her husband were raising a family in Denver, Colorado. She was working on a concept for a new and different K–8 school. This school would be based on entrepreneurial principles of leadership, risk taking, accountability, decision making, and creating a business. Along the way she became a single mom but continued to pursue her dream and raise her family. She started the Aspen Academy in Littleton, Colorado.

I met her when I was invited to give a speech to a group of EOers and YPOers at her school auditorium. I spent the day with Kristina learning everything about the school. It was amazing! The students and faculty were alive with energy and enthusiasm. Every one of them knew the vision statement by memory, and they could also recite all the values of the school. Additionally, the students were involved in managing some of the school's most vital functions, the cafeteria and the bookstore. Each student had to write a business plan and start a business by the time they graduated from eighth grade. Among her strongest supporters are the business leaders in her area.

The Aspen Academy is extraordinary. It has become the epicenter for new ideas in education, and Kristina, a woman who leads others to create purposeful lives by example, is considered one of the most exceptional educators in the United States. She is a good friend and someone to whom I listen with real intensity. I always learn from her.

To lead anyone or anything with greatness and soul, one must first master leading themselves. This mastery requires a steadfast commitment to the intentionality of one's personal, family, business, and community life. Warren Rustand is quite simply a true leadership expert. His thinking, saying, being, and doing is an exemplar that sets the high-water mark and provides the evidence of the positive and productive impact one person can make on tens of thousands of people and how that can affect the many generations thereafter. Warren's habits, practices, stories, and sage perspective provide an inspiring and pragmatic path toward achieving your highest and best self. Warren is simply the wisest and kindest of leaders and mentors that I've ever known.

—**Kristina Scala, Founder and President of Aspen Academy Future Holders MODI**

The Importance of a Personal Vision Statement

We've all heard of a vision statement, but we probably haven't created our own because we don't know how, or we don't have clarity of what it is or how to do it. We don't actually know where we are going. In fact, most of us end up living lives by serendipity, not by design. We are living a reactive life, not a proactive one. Luckily, we can change that and create a personal vision statement that will guide our lives.

You might be thinking, *What's a personal vision statement anyway? Does it have to be a long, eloquent paragraph I'm supposed to memorize?* No, it doesn't have to be long, nor do you have to memorize it. I'm not asking you to create a dissertation. It can be as long or as brief as it needs to be to fully convey your overall vision, so write a statement that's meaningful to you.

A vision statement should be both aspirational and inspirational. It should be a part of your life both directionally and philosophically. It is the long-range intent of your life. At times it can be a

> A vision statement should be both aspirational and inspirational. It should be a part of your life both directionally and philosophically.

destination, but most often it is the distant landmark against which you measure your progress.

My *personal* vision statement is simple: "To improve the human condition wherever I find it." It means instead of making judgments about people and circumstances, extending a hand of fellowship, a kind word, an interest in others, and physical help where I can. It is to be aware of my environment and see needs in which I can play a part. That applies to the homeless, the person waiting tables, the person making the bed in a hotel room, and to our family and extended family. I do my best to be vigilant to the needs of others. I am not perfect in this regard, but I work at it every day.

I've had my vision statement for decades now. And it's directed my career and how I invest and why I invest in, or choose not to invest in, certain companies. Because of what I believe, "to improve the human condition wherever I find it," I choose to pursue companies that elevate people within and without the companies, and spend time working with not-for-profits that help other people improve their life condition.

It's also directed me in my personal life, and our family's life, in giving service to others, helping others. That's something that our family has been doing since we first married. We all have the opportunity and capacity to change or save lives; all it takes is our desire and commitment to do so. All the members of our family are so committed.

For all of you reading this book, we are the fortunate ones who live in abundance compared to others, and who have great ability to give to others. Why not start now?

Creating Your Vision Statement

When you begin the process of crafting your personal vision statement, the goal is to create something that is unique and not so general that it sounds like it could be for anyone. All too often, people draft grandiose vision statements that are so general they're almost meaningless: "I want to save the world," "I want my life to be amazing."

I'm not saying these aren't good goals, but they're so vague that there's no way to gauge whether you're doing the work. There's no specific metric to attain or direction in which to focus your efforts. So, take the time to create something that's specific to you.

Step One: Time and Space

What we encourage people to do first is to create time and space in their always-busy lives so they can really think and reflect on their vision. What is the alignment between your vision and purpose? This is my purpose; therefore, this is where I am going. It creates momentum and forward movement both directionally and philosophically.

Making the time to think and find a relaxing place in which to do this mental exercise is the beginning of your vision statement. You can do this at a park, mountaintop, beach, or on a hike, or other places to clear your mind, but try to find peace and tranquility. Wherever it is, make sure you're alone so you're able to maintain your focus and not be influenced by the thoughts, noise, and opinions of others.

Step Two: What is Your Purpose?

Next, what do you think about when you have the time and space to let your mind wander and relax? What is your purpose and passion? If you could do anything, what would it be? If you could create your future, clean sheet of paper, blue sky, open ocean, what would that look like? You can begin to link words together that are key indicators: joy, happiness, purpose, passion, self-worth, service, commitment, and love.

When you can begin to think about things that you do well, things that you want to learn to do or enjoy, you discover your vision.

Step Three: What Are You Passionate About?

The third step is then to begin to write down words that describe that passion, that joy, or that happiness. What are the things that you do that bring a smile to your face and a sense of great satisfaction? What would you do whether or not you got paid? Don't worry about spelling or grammar, or if you're writing down too many words or not enough. Let yourself brainstorm without judgment and capture your thoughts.

Step Four: Distill the Essence

Once you've written down as many words as you can think of that describe your purpose and passions, the fourth step is to begin to eliminate some of those words. You need to distill and refine them until you get a succinct group of words.

Then you begin to create phrases, or concepts, using those words that describe your passion, your purpose, what it is you'd be doing if you could do anything.

You'll delete and refine that list again and again until you have *a statement or two* that really fits you. It isn't meant to fit anyone else—it fits you, and it's as unique as you are. And when you read your statement, it will resonate with you to your core.

I encourage you to keep your personal vision statement available at all times, and to have it somewhere where you can see and review it on a regular basis.

Building Family Vision and Values Statements

When we started building our family vision statement, we went through the same exercise as we did in creating a personal vision and values statement, except we involved the entire family in the creation of the vision statement. First, we chose words that described our family, then we distilled all the words into concepts and then into sentences. Ultimately, there were five concepts important to our family that made it into the final vision statement: "An eternally sealed family that helps each member reach their potential through unconditional love and respect for differences, where all are committed to lead Christ-centered lives, and that serves as a protective shield for all within."

We have our vision statement by our front door and our value statement by our back door. Our family vision statement has never been revised, and no one's ever wanted to change a single word of it. If you read those two statements, then you understand where we are going and how we live together.

Because these statements are part of our daily lives, they are great prompts for having a meaningful discussion with our children. We can talk to our children about decisions they are making and how they relate to where the family is going and see whether there is alignment.

The vision statement is where you are going, and the companion piece is the values statement, which is how you will behave during your journey.

For your *values statement*, you can use a similar process to the one that was described earlier, but be sure to involve the entire family. If the children have ownership of the end product, it is likely that you will have more adherence to the values created for the family.

There are nine items on our family values list. They have helped us navigate our everyday lives and actions.

A Worthwhile Investment of Time

The time we give to the creation of these three documents for our lives is very important. Personal and family vision statements, with the companion values statement, will serve as keystones for the duration of our lives. They are the alignment and unification of our hearts, minds, and souls in common understandings about the scope and worth of our lives.

Life is premeditation, not chance. Success comes as we are proactive in all aspects of our lives.

Let's remember what Stephen Covey wrote about in his book *The 7 Habits of Highly Successful People* and what we discussed earlier in this book. He said there are three great moments of truth in a person's life. The first is when they decide in their heart and their soul who they really are, their core beliefs and values. The second is when they commit to their core beliefs and values. And the third is to act on those core beliefs and values. When we experience these three moments of truth, we can be sure that we are living with purpose, acting with intent, and doing so in alignment with our values.

CHAPTER 7

THE THIRD PRINCIPLE OF PERSONAL GREATNESS: ACTING WITH INTENT

Only the disciplined ones are free in life. If you aren't disciplined, you are a slave to your moods. You are a slave to your passions.
—Eliud Kipchoge

Intentionality matters. The ability and capacity to act with real thought and planning make a big difference in all things we are trying to accomplish. Our intent needs to be tied to and a part of our vision.

What is the distant landmark against which we are measuring our progress, and are we acting on it intentionally with the many activities in which we are engaged? In the rush of our present-day society, are we actually getting to the priorities of our lives, or are we satisfied to just get our "to-do list" completed? We talk so much about the stress, pressure, and frenetic pace of our lives that we feel like we are just surviving rather than living out our life by design through our intentional acts.

Once we have clarity of vision, meaning we understand where we are going, then planning out our daily, weekly, monthly, and longer-term schedules with intent turns our wishes into accomplishments. It is a short but important step from dreaming to actualization. From thinking to doing. This can be best done by having a specific, disciplined process by which one determines their priorities and then executes a well-thought-out plan to get them done.

Each day should be approached with intent. Rather than getting swept along in a series of unintentional activities, not really knowing the why or what of the events, why not carefully chart out the way in which you will execute your day? When done, this gives you self-confidence, certainty, and self-worth around your plan and outcomes. Every day becomes one of many important milestones being achieved as great progress is being made. This is a life of forward momentum and success.

Ten Rules for Effective Time Management

I teach time management a great deal because people are often overwhelmed with the minutiae of the everyday; they are looking to regain control of their time in order to accomplish and enjoy life more.

People often look at my life and wonder how I've accomplished as much as I have. They see the results of a lifetime of work and discipline and perhaps want a quick fix. I have a wonderful wife, seven children, and nineteen grandchildren; I work hard to be an active husband, father, grandfather, business leader, community volunteer, and still take care of myself. So it's not uncommon for people to ask me, "How did you do all that stuff? How do you get so much done?" The truth is that it takes a lot of work and discipline.

I really learned about time when I was working in the White House and scheduling the president's time. In creating his schedule, there are implications for scores of other people who must react and respond to his commitments and activities. Any meeting or trip might activate anywhere from ten to fifteen hundred people. You see, when we schedule our time, we aren't just acting for ourselves alone, but we act as leaders, wives or husbands, mothers or fathers. Time commitments we make have implications for others, oftentimes many others. When it comes to time, we must understand that the decisions we make don't just affect us.

Below are the ten rules for effective time management.

1. Recognize and act on the knowledge that the root cause of poor use of your time is poor habits.

2. Recognize and act on the knowledge that you must control your time or others will control it for you.

3. Recognize and act on the knowledge that you can only spend time; you can't save it.

4. Recognize and act on the knowledge that it is necessary to learn to say no.

5. Recognize and act on the knowledge that if you don't have time to plan, you cannot work efficiently.

6. Recognize and act on the knowledge that you must organize your time or lose it.

7. Recognize and act on the knowledge of the dollar value of your time.

8. Recognize and act on the knowledge that your greatest asset in life in achieving your goals is time.

9. Recognize and act on the knowledge that it will require continued courage on your part to defeat the time wasters.

10. Recognize and act on the knowledge that the key to successful time management is to build good time management systems and act within them.

Acting with intent, especially when it comes to time management, is a simple idea in theory, but harder to put into practice—at least at first. However, the longer you are in control of your own time, the easier it becomes to protect that time and to set boundaries.

When I was the appointments secretary to President Gerald Ford, I helped, with others, to manage the president's time. We quickly discovered that he received hundreds, if not thousands, of invitations for his time each week. Each communication was important. They came from kings, queens, prime ministers, members of Congress, old and new friends, and so on. What my staff and I had to do most was to say *no* to people because he didn't have enough time to say *yes* to all of the invitations.

After several weeks of declining invitations on his behalf, Don Rumsfeld, Dick Cheney, and I talked about a different approach to scheduling. If the president could state with clarity his highest level of priorities for his administration and his presidency, then we could begin to schedule on a proactive rather than a reactive basis. The president did just that.

Scheduling for the president is always difficult. There are many competing interests and issues to be considered. There are both mandatory and voluntary commitments. However, when one looks at the Ford presidency, one sees that he accomplished a great deal, specifically on the most significant issues of his day. When one evaluates his foreign, national security, economic, and domestic policies, one sees he had an outstanding term of office. He was able to do that because of his laser-like focus on what was most important. He had many exceptional people around him who helped him gain clarity and intent on those critical priorities.

Important to that is the idea that every minute of every day counts. Time is not something with which one can be frivolous. Shakespeare said it well. "Money is not the coin of the realm. Time is the coin of the realm."

> Every minute of every day counts. Time is not something with which one can be frivolous.

Four Buckets: Family, Business, Community, Self

About ten years ago, I gave a speech in Jetta, Saudi Arabia, to about three hundred members of EO, all of whom were CEOs. In that speech I spoke about the totality of the entrepreneurial leader, the 360-degree leader. I indicated that almost everything we do falls into four buckets: family, business, community, and self. This four-bucket system is a way of determining priorities, managing hours, and driving outcomes on a daily basis. It helps to establish the highest level of priority for each of the buckets and then base your schedule on those highest priorities. When setting priorities, another important element is whether or not the goal is attainable. Establishing appropriate expectations for oneself is essential for our priorities.

Many people miss out on their potential for greatness. They have a great vision, such as "I want to be a basketball player," but they forget that they have to run drills and shoot hundreds of shots every day. There's a big gap between saying, "I want to be this" and actually executing on the vision every single day. Bobby Knight, a legendary basketball coach, told us that "the key is not the will to win. Everybody has that. It is the will to prepare to win that is important." A person must do all the things that create success—and not just think about being successful.

Over many years of working with high achievers and successful individuals, from presidents and world leaders to CEOs, and everyone in between, I've developed a time management system that helps define the top three priorities for success in each of the four buckets of life. I currently mentor thirty-five CEOs, and most of them use this system for time efficiency and effectiveness.

There are four buckets in our life: For me, family is first, business is second, community is third, and *I am* fourth. Almost everything we do fits into one of those four buckets. What's important is that we define our highest three priorities in each of those four buckets.

You will have twelve priorities, three for each bucket, and many milestones that must be hit in order for you to achieve all of your priorities. For each priority, write specific milestones that you must complete in order to accomplish that priority. Then write a date next to it by which that milestone must be completed.

Read your list of priorities at least once a week. Do this so that you keep your mind focused on those things you have decided are the most important to accomplish in your life.

Then transfer all of the milestones with a date next to them to a separate sheet of paper or a different place on your computer. Each week place them in order by the date by which they are to be accomplished. This is called your core schedule. These many milestones become a part of your daily schedule.

While you can't work on all twelve priorities in a day (or sometimes even in a week), you can choose several milestones each day by which to plan your daily schedule. By doing this, you are always working on some of your highest priorities each and every day. As you complete all the milestones under each priority, you will have achieved that particular priority, and you will be prepared to add a new one.

In my family bucket, let's say spending more time with my wife is my number-one priority. Therefore, the three milestones I list under this are: Have a date night each Friday; take a three-day driving trip each quarter; and take two one-week vacations a year, six months apart, to places she chooses. These milestones should help me accomplish my highest family priority.

In my business bucket, I may want to make an acquisition my highest priority. I then list all the milestones necessary to achieve it with dates certain for each milestone. Then I transfer all of the milestones to my core schedule from which I create my daily schedule.

Remember, it is not necessary to work on every priority every day. Work on the milestones by the date by which they need to be completed. Therefore, you are making progress on your highest priorities every day.

It is necessary to be very specific about creating and enjoying a designed life. Every morning I remind myself, *This is where I want to go, and this is how I'm going to get there.* And then I act on that every day.

I learned to schedule my time by scheduling for the president of the United States. At that level every second is important and accounted for—it's all committed. And it's challenging to deal with so many difficult and different issues. The only issues put before the president are big issues. Others take care of the small things. I encourage you to implement the same levels of decision making in your own business.

An important consideration in creating our priorities is an understanding of the need for flexibility and adaptability. From time to time, there will be illness, death, failure, or other urgencies that will take us off track. When that happens, and it will, we just need to recalibrate, adjust, and get back on track. It is all a part of the process of success.

You're the visionary leader of your business. You need to stay focused on those 86,400 seconds each day. They are all you get before the next day starts, again.

Annual Priorities

Business

	Completion Date:
Priority 1: _____	_____
• _____	_____
• _____	_____
• _____	

	Completion Date:
Priority 2: _____	_____
• _____	_____
• _____	_____
• _____	

	Completion Date:
Priority 3: _____	_____
• _____	_____
• _____	_____
• _____	

Surviving and Thriving after Chernobyl: The Story of Natalia Matveeva

I met Natalia Matveeva at the Global Leadership Academy in 2011 and subsequently accepted her invitation to visit Moscow nearly ten years ago. She was the leader of a group of CEOs, members of EO, in Russia, and she had invited me to speak to the group. As I got to know her and her husband, I began to understand her remarkable story.

She and her twin sister were seven years old, her mother a doctor and father a ship captain, when they became part of a global story. They were in Chernobyl, Russia, on an exchange and were due to live there for only six months. Her family lived just a mile from the Chernobyl nuclear power plant the day that one of the nuclear reactors melted down and exploded, sending radiation around the globe.

All who know about the Chernobyl incident know of the unbelievable devastation that extended out from Chernobyl for hundreds of miles, killing men, women, children, and animals, and defoliating the entire area over an extended period of time.

The day following the accident, Soviet troops came to vacate the town and rescue everyone, including Natalia and her family. They were taken to another location, where they were washed and cleansed from the radiation to which they had been exposed. Several days later they were taken to a hospital.

Natalia, not to be deterred, continued on her path of learning and growing, ultimately graduating from her university. She wanted to be an entrepreneur and had an idea of building a gaming company. Not knowing if she would live for very long because of her exposure to radiation, she was in a hurry and had a sense of urgency. She had enormous energy and intellect, and she built a significant gaming company, which included some of the most popular casual games in the world. She sold her gaming company when in her midthirties. She's currently building her second company, a healthcare company that when completed will have application across the entire globe. The app is in beta testing at this time. It will help detect anemia in children.

Over the years we have known each other, we have had the occasion to talk about the important principles of leading a life by design and the way in which she should think about herself in the world and how to interact with that world. We have discussed the interesting opportunities that have presented themselves to her and given her unique perspective, skills, and abilities, and how she could apply that which she knows and wants to do to benefit others and the world.

She is an amazing spiritual being; she is a wonderful woman, a special friend, and has proven that one can go through the most trying and difficult times not knowing why she lived, and then not knowing how long she will live, but living every day with a growth mindset.

She is leading an intentional life. She is healthy, she is vibrant, she is exceptional, and she is making a contribution to the world. She has embraced the very principles we are discussing—clarity of vision, certainty of intent, power of values and of living every day with discipline, purpose, intent, choice, and cause. These can govern one's life and, when applied, alter one's life. It'll be exciting to see what she does for the world in the years ahead as she makes every minute count and counts every minute.

If you want to practice leadership based on virtue—this is your book. If you want to lead on unity—this is your book. If you want to serve the world and not just a few—this is your book. This book holds together years of experience of leading and teaching entrepreneurs in any part of the world, from any culture and background. It holds the principles to build a world leader from ground zero. This book is applicable for all and at all times.

—Natalia Matveeva, CEO of Probiovita

Stay Focused on Your Own Agenda

In Stephen Covey's book *The 7 Habits of Highly Successful People*, he separates his view of time into four quadrants. The quadrant he urges us to spend time in is quadrant two, which is doing the important, not the urgent. If we regularly spend our time doing that which is urgent, we have difficulty getting to the important, and the important is what drives our life.

	Urgent	Not Urgent
Important	Q1	Q2
Not Important	Q3	Q4

There will always be those urgent needs that require our attention, such as an email, phone call, or text, and they interrupt our daily flow. The average text seems to be responded to in about thirty seconds. The average email is responded to in minutes. If we're responding in that way, we're just working on other people's motivations and agendas. We're not working on our own agenda; we are being reactive, not proactive. That's where most of us are today—we're responding, not initiating.

What if somebody stops by your office and wants to see you? I have an open-door policy, and I can tell you that people always walk through the door. They always want us, and we always want to respond because it makes us feel good to be the decision maker, the smartest one in the room. But if we're not careful, we'll find a lot of people coming through our door, and pretty soon we're simply acting on *their* agenda, not our agenda.

> People who empower other people become even better and stronger leaders. The people who are empowered respect their leaders and become leaders themselves.

The key is in allowing them to be their own decision makers and changemakers. If we empower our colleagues to make decisions and find solutions, we'll still have to deal with urgent matters now and then, but we'll soon find fewer people walking through our door. People who empower other people become even better and stronger leaders. The people who are empowered respect their leaders and become leaders themselves.

Being more productive will require a change in behavior. So, the first thing I do when I am mentoring a CEO is to do a time log. We write down every activity each day and put it in one of four buckets: family, business, community, self.

We have 168 hours per week. About one third of that time is spent sleeping, so what we do with the balance of our time is important.

We keep the time log for three weeks, then break down each bucket by total hours and percentage of time, reviewing them to see how they are actually spending their time. Then we analyze the results with an eye toward finding the right rhythm and pace for each person. We look for opportunities to save time in specific areas and use that time in new or different ways that will enable the CEO to become more effective. And you can do this exact exercise in your own life to recapture your time.

Jeff Neufeld, CEO of TriMet, an EO member from Calgary, Canada, thought he was doing a pretty good job of managing his time. Yet, after completing the time log analysis, he could see there was a very big opportunity for improvement and change. Now that he has made those alterations, each of the four buckets has gotten significantly better. His life is very different today than it was just two years ago.

He is a much more present husband and father, spending more time with his family and in family activities. He has changed the style and substance of his leadership of his company. He has focused on being an attentive leader, building a people-first corporate culture, and has increased revenue and profitability significantly. He has focused his efforts in the community and has begun to make a real impact for others and his company. Lastly, he has a morning routine, has stopped drinking, has lost thirty pounds, and is in the best shape of his life.

One of the hardest parts of entrepreneurship is defining success and knowing when I've done enough. Warren Rustand has helped me realize that I find it when I reach slightly beyond my competence, stretch just past my limits, and strive outside of my comfort zone, with a sense of joy and adventure every day, and do so as a father, a husband, a community member, and a leader. I feel I'm redefining my potential and testing my outer limits every single day.

—Jeff Neufeld, CEO of Neuhoff Capital

Yes, there are hundreds of time management systems, electronic and paper. They all have some beneficial impact, but how do you actually get to your highest level of priorities? And how do you schedule around those higher-level priorities so that every day you are only working on your highest-level issues? You build your schedule the same way a president does! At the end of your day, week, month, and year, you will have accomplished much more.

Act with intent. Don't be unintentional about life—your time, your actions, and your words. We're here, on average, for about seventy-five to eighty years. In the history of the world, that is only a nanosecond in time.

Every day is important.

Every hour is important.

Every minute is important.

Let's make the most and the best use of our time while on planet Earth.

CHAPTER 8

THE FOURTH PRINCIPLE OF PERSONAL GREATNESS: MAKING CONSCIOUS CHOICES

We have to dream, but we must plan.
We have to believe, but we must act.

Conscious choice is the decision to act with the full understanding of what each action means, including the consequences that follow. While it is not possible to always see with exactness the complete outcome of each decision, it is possible to have an understanding of the ramifications of our choice.

We do understand the difference between good and bad. The opposite of that unconscious choice is the idea that we develop the herd mentality. We go along with others without thinking about the consequences of our choices. We get swept along with emotion or momentum. We go with the crowd rather than deliberately making a choice to do. In order to avoid the herd mentality, we must often stand alone in what we believe to be right for us.

Ricky Hunley understands conscious choice. Ricky grew up in the projects in Petersburg, Virginia. He had a very strong, demanding, and present mother, Miss Scarlet. None of the ten children called her Mom. While raising her children, she also had some sixty foster children. Her admonition: Never lie to me, and give your best.

Ricky made a choice to pursue athletics. By the end of high school, he was a widely recruited baseball and football player. He was offered scholarships to most of the biggest universities in the United States. He chose the University of Arizona, where he played football over baseball, and where he became a two-time consensus All-American linebacker. At that time, he was the second-youngest player ever chosen for the NCAA College Football Hall of Fame. He was the seventh player taken in the first round of the NFL draft in 1984. He played seven years in the NFL, including two Super Bowls. He coached at the university and NFL level for over twenty-two years. He currently lives in Los Angeles with his family, where he works in advertising.

I met Ricky when he was a nineteen-year-old student-athlete at Arizona. We consider him one of our sons. He spent a great deal of time at our home while in college. Our family loves him and his brothers, and they love our family. Ricky is a good example for others, as he made important and conscious choices that determined his life path.

It is with great pleasure that I get to share some of my thoughts and feelings about an amazing man, Warren Rustand. Over the past thirty-six years, I have been very fortunate to have Warren in my life, as a life coach, mentor, and great friend. Warren has developed the necessary skills to teach without preaching and gently steer others in the direction of service to others for the greater good. He has mastered the art of attacking opportunities with a single focus and a single purpose. I truly believe that the teachings of Warren Rustand will live on forever. This must-read book by Warren has packed tons of wisdom into just a few words.

—Ricky Hunley, Former NFL player and coach

Voices and Choices

In today's society we are bombarded with millions of stimuli each day. It sometimes seems impossible to sift and sort among all the marketplace noise that is coming at us. It requires thoughtful consideration of the many things we are trying to get done in our lives. The noise always seems to get in the way. Family, friends, colleagues, social media, television, music, and the general environmental considerations all have an impact on our minds and, therefore, ultimately our choices.

> Sift out the noise, make conscious choices, and be intentional. We decide to which voices we will listen, and we decide what choices we will make.

To be strong, constant, and consistent is often very difficult. Yet, those who are leaders, high achievers, and exceptional people all seem to have figured it out. Sift out the noise, make conscious choices, and be intentional. We decide to which voices we will listen, and we decide what choices we will make.

Strategy Is Everything

As we sort through all the noise in our lives, we begin to have clarity of vision. Following our vision is our certainty of intent. This is our strategy for action on our vision. Strategy matters. Our strategies are what we are going to do and how we will do it. They are specific statements of our intent. Life is not chance, it is premeditation. We can be great at execution, but if we are executing against a flawed strategy, we will not succeed. We cannot simply hope good things will happen to us; we must strategize and plan out how we will execute our lives. This applies to all four buckets—family, business, community, and self.

The question is, how much time do you spend thinking about strategies for your life? This is fundamental to making conscious choices.

I spend two hours per day, so ten hours a week, in concentrated strategy sessions. On most days, at 10:00 a.m. and again at 2:00 p.m., I close my door, turn off my technology, and for an hour I focus on specific topics that require strategic thinking. The thinking might include making an acquisition, being a better father, helping a not-for-profit, or reading about personal development. It depends on what is happening in my life that requires me to give deeper thought to a subject and from which a strategy for intentional action occurs.

Your decision to spend time on strategic, conscious choices will dramatically alter your life. Make a conscious choice to make strategic thinking part of your formal agenda each day. Strategic thinking and conscious choice affect every aspect of your life.

The Top One Hundred

I have performed pretty well from an early age. I owe much of that to my dad, who filled my mind with knowledge and possibility as we were driving the tractor, and who showed me a model of hard work and effort. But performing at a high level has gotten much easier as I began to understand the wider implications of my actions and goals, and then began to work them through.

My father had impressed upon me the ideas around goal setting when I was graduating from high school and entering college. Sometime during my second year at the University of Arizona, I was struck with the thought that I should create a list of the things I wanted to do in my life. I felt so compelled that I sat down and did so almost immediately. So, I wrote my list of the one hundred things I wanted to accomplish in my life.

As you can imagine, some were young and innocent and others more challenging and dramatic. I have looked at that list nearly every week for the last fifty-eight years as a reminder of what I want to do in my life. I made a conscious choice to make the list and acted with intentionality to do the things listed. What I found was that by looking at it regularly, I was reminded of my goals, and by so doing I tended to act on those goals.

I have completed ninety-eight of the one hundred items on the list. There are two that I won't likely get done. One is that I wanted to visit every country recognized by the United Nations. Countries get divided and names changed, so it's a moving target; however, I have visited most of the countries in the world.

Second, I wanted to be president of the United States; however, I may have missed my chance. Perhaps, if I had run four years ago, I'd have had a solid shot!

About twenty years ago, I made another list of one hundred things, and I have done about half of that list.

> Lead a life by your design. Your heart already knows what you want; now go do that.

So why don't you make your list? Decide what it is you want to do during the rest of your life. Take control of your life, and make conscious choices. Lead a life by your design. Your heart already knows what you want; now go do that.

Prevailing over Cancer:
The Story of Mary Leonida

Mary lives in Kansas City; she's a member of EO, a global entrepreneurs organization, which is how we met. She is an absolute sweetheart, and everyone who knows her loves her greatly. She has been a wonderful friend for many years.

Mary was running a successful real estate and restaurant business. She was also one of the strongest leaders in Kansas City for the performing arts. And she has chaired just about every not-for-profit associated with the arts in her city. She raised money, organized events, and committed herself to making sure the arts were strong and powerful for children's programs and the community.

On a routine visit to her doctor, she was given a diagnosis of cancer. It surprised her, as she was young and vibrant, but she knew she had to deal with it, so she called me, and we talked. We had been talking ever since I first met her, and she had changed her life in ways that allowed her to be more disciplined, better organized, more purposeful. But now she knew she was in the fight of her life. Mary was committed to battling this sinister illness with her whole heart and soul.

In the process of doing that, she sold her business so she could concentrate on the battle. There have been complications. There has been surgery. It has been a difficult and challenging road for the last four years.

Mary has been a real warrior princess. She did everything she could do within her control. She applied the principles of vision, intent, values, mindset, discipline, positive thinking, and commitment to outcomes. She has prevailed and is doing very well. She started a consulting business and is soon to buy another business and start again as CEO.

We wish her well and I admire all who engage in the battle against cancer.

Without question, Warren's instruction has had an immensely positive impact during both my life's gratifying highlights and its serious challenges. As I applied his foundational leadership principles, I came to realize their enduring value provided the clarity and discipline that I really needed not only to survive but also to thrive in all circumstances. In addition, Warren's principles provided me with the ability to identify my true intent and accordingly to execute difficult but essential business/personal decisions. I'm certain that this book will serve as a valuable reference guide for me and countless others. Hopefully for many readers, it also will reinforce Warren's concept of engagement in a greater cause, which for me has become one of the most important principles of application for happiness and gratitude in my life.

—**Mary Leonida, CEO, Regional Consulting Firm**

CHAPTER 9

THE FIFTH PRINCIPLE OF PERSONAL GREATNESS: ENGAGING IN A CAUSE GREATER THAN SELF

There is a destiny which makes us sisters and brothers;
no one goes through life alone. All that we give into
the lives of others comes back into our own.

—**Edwin Markham**

The fifth principle of personal greatness is to be engaged in a cause greater than self. It's the giving of our time, talent, and energy to something in which we believe.

When we personally are going through challenging times and feeling a bit down, the best way to work our way out of it is to serve someone else. The magic is to forget about ourselves and help someone whose circumstance is more difficult than our own. It helps our perspective.

More Than Money

I believe engaging in a cause greater than self is more than just writing a check. Financial contributions are important, necessary, and a wonderful form of generosity. But could we be doing more?

When we've written a check to a worthy cause, we sometimes feel like that's enough—we've checked the box and used our own resources to help someone. But perhaps our time, talents, and energy are more important than our money. Money is the relatively easy part of giving, but oftentimes serving and taking action are needed even more. The result for us can be profound.

I hope to push people to engage. To commit. To devote time. Because when we bring our time, talents, and energy, it changes the nature of the cause and the nature of our involvement. *We* grow and the organization grows as well.

Lift Where You Stand

My wife is a classic example of service and engaging in causes dear to her and to our family. She sees the world not in terms of "I, me, and my" but as "we, ours, and us." Life is about everybody else, *then us.* She wakes up every day smiling, wanting to know how she can serve other people. She has been involved in very important and worthwhile causes over her lifetime, for example: early childhood education, educational enrichment, spousal and child abuse, child advocacy for the Superior Court, immigrant education and citizenship, homelessness, and at-risk families. All of this she has done cheerfully and happily.

For several years she has been working with immigrants to teach them English and get them ready to be American citizens. She has served as a shining example of community commitment and involvement. All of our children and grandchildren are, likewise, engaged in causes greater than themselves. As a family we believe that's the way we should live our lives, and it represents a vital part of our purpose.

For me, my wife embodies the concept "lift where you stand." The quote comes from Dieter F. Uchtdorf, a German pilot, airline executive, and religious leader. The notion is, wherever we are in our lives, we lift those people around us up to a higher level. Sometimes that's done with a handshake. Sometimes it's a smile. Sometimes it's a hug. Sometimes it's an interest in what they're doing. Sometimes it's calling them by name so they feel seen. And sometimes it's working shoulder to shoulder with them to do something special. Our purpose as a family is to acknowledge and recognize all people regardless of their status or station in life. We want to eliminate the notion of invisible people, those we pass by every day without respecting them as individuals within our environment.

We want people who associate with us to feel our presence in an uplifting way. It doesn't matter with whom we associate—we will, in fact, do our best to lift those people to a higher level. So, lift where you stand. Regardless of where we find ourselves standing in life, we can lift others up with acts of kindness and generosity of spirit.

Let me share with you an idea that was given to me by Lysset Butler and her mother on how to recognize people who help us. Each time I check out of a hotel, I leave a $20 bill with a handwritten note that says, "Thank you very much for making my stay comfortable," and I sign my name. On several occasions, I've forgotten something in the room, and I've gone back to get whatever I have left behind. A few times, the person who serviced my room is standing there holding the note and the money. When I've asked them what's more important to them, what do you think they've said? *The note is always more important.*

Many people who are cleaning rooms and making beds are

entry-level employees or new to our country. Their jobs, like ours, are essential to the welfare of their family. When someone expresses appreciation for their work, the simple notion that they have been respected helps their self-esteem and self-respect.

When we are not focused on a greater cause, we tend to become more myopic in our view. It is easy to fall into a life centered on ourselves and our needs. Social media, specifically, can move us in the direction of a more narcissistic space, focused on how many likes and followers we have based on our pictures, opinions, and videos. We get caught up in creating a profile—a curated version of ourselves we want the world to see. Then we begin to believe we *are* the profile. And we create this false sense of reality for everyone to see.

But that's all the more reason to truly connect with others *outside* of social media. We have a big life to live and to serve as we share with others!

My observation is that the greatest gift we receive from helping others is humility. And I believe that is the most important quality of outstanding leaders.

The second is the ability to listen.

The third is to be a good communicator.

The fourth is to have EQ (emotional quotient).

And the fifth is IQ.

When we review this list of top qualities of outstanding leaders, they're the very kinds of attributes we learn by serving others. I believe serving others is one of the ways we define a successful life.

We need to respect all people. Everywhere and in all places. Elevate people to a higher level. Be that transformational leader. Do the small things that matter to others.

The next time you're out for a meal and somebody is serving you, be gracious to them. Ask them what they're doing, why they're doing it. Show an interest. Respect them. We collectively elevate the people around us. Whether it's walking into the convenience store, helping a colleague at work, or starting a conversation with somebody who is helping us with our car, let's elevate people. Let's lift where we stand. If we do that, we change the world one life at a time.

When it's all said and done, it's about helping other people. All of us have the power to save at least one life.

The Story of Steve Satterwhite

After graduating from college, Steve worked in corporate settings until he decided to start his own company. Over the past two decades, his IT staffing company, Entelligence, has grown steadily; today it is a multi-million-dollar organization employing some two hundred people.

I have known Steve for several years, but about three years ago he called and asked if he could visit me at my home. We spent the first hour with tears in our eyes as he told me about his family dysfunction growing up, which had led to a lack of self-esteem and self-worth today. He had just come through a very difficult divorce, and he was battling other addictions and distractions that kept him from his true potential. Mostly, he was worried for their three children, whom he dearly loved.

His business was stagnating, as he had been an absent CEO, and he had some challenges with his business partner. In short, his life was in a very difficult place. He wanted, and needed, to change. Along the way he told me of his desire to help veterans, minorities, and women find jobs in the IT space. He even wrote a book about his vision for using his company as a vehicle of change that would benefit thousands of people in marginalized communities not present or represented in the IT world.

We spent hours talking not only about clarity of vision, certainty of intent, and the power of values but also, importantly, how each applied to the various aspects of his life and how he could change his current state. Based on those principles, we began to formulate plans for every aspect of his life: family, business, community, and self. Then he began the transformative change process.

So, what happened? How did it work for Steve? He made peace with his childhood trauma and developed a good relationship with his former wife. He has deepened his bonds with his children. He completely reinvented his business, building a self-directed work group corporate design, incentive-based high performance systems, and a caring and nurturing culture.

Now he is growing his revenue more than 50 percent per year. He is engaging his community in new ways and has created a highly collaborative and consensual leadership style.

He has given up his bad habits, replaced them with new habits, and has focused on yoga, meditation, nutrition, and physical conditioning. He has reinvested his time in his most important relationships, those with his children and closest friends. In his words: "I am the happiest I have ever been." The key is that he became a servant to others. He assisted others in finding their happiness, and in so doing he found his own. Steve is an exceptional leader, great father, and wonderful friend.

Warren's timeless wisdom on leadership is not just about business but can be applied to every area of life. Since working with Warren and following his formula for success, my business has doubled in size and value, my relationships with my family and friends are deeper and more authentic, and my own personal health has never been better. I could say that I wish I had met Warren years ago. But, as the saying goes, "when the student is ready, the teacher appears." Warren is that teacher for me. And I truly believe his model for leadership is one that is sorely needed in the world now.

—Steve Satterwhite, CEO, Entelligence

The Power of Servant Leadership: Dr. Malik Mohammed

I met Malik and his wife, Christina, in 2013 in a small school in Delaware. I was the new CEO of Providence Service Corporation, a billion-dollar, publicly traded healthcare services company. I had heard of Malik and his innovative educational practices, which were having a wonderful effect and driving successful outcomes for young students who found it impossible to be in a traditional classroom. What I witnessed Malik and Christina doing with young children and the results they were getting were remarkable. You see, Malik could relate.

Malik was first arrested when he was only ten years old. He spent much of the next few years in and out of detention centers. He struggled to feel connected to school. He was angry, frustrated, and difficult. He and his family spent six years homeless, often living in the back of a U-Haul truck.

When he was about fifteen, a teacher and coach took a special interest in him, which started a new and different period of his life. He converted to Islam. He became a better student, graduated from high school, and started on his undergraduate degree. His girlfriend, Christina, became pregnant, they got married, and they both earned their degrees on time from a prestigious college. Malik and Christina both went on to get masters' and doctorates in education and psychology while raising two beautiful children.

What they discovered was that by serving others, often the more underserved and marginalized, they became better people themselves. Their capacity for giving to others is legendary.

Malik and I have the chance to teach and present each year at the Global Entrepreneurial Leadership Academy in Washington, DC, where I serve as the dean of learning. I have the greatest respect and admiration for both Malik and Christina. I consider Malik to be one of my best friends and a great example of a servant leader.

Witnessing Warren's leadership and presence in action, it is clear that he is guided by a deep sense of purpose and conviction in a values-driven path. Many of us who know him well have been inspired to radically show up better in our own families, companies, communities, and faiths. I know that I have. With this book, Warren shares with a broader audience the principles that he has been practicing and teaching to many, including stubborn but growing leaders like me, for years.

—Dr. Malik Muhammad, Founder and CEO, Akoben LLC and Transforming Lives Inc.

The idea of servant leadership was first written about in 1977 in a book titled *Servant Leadership*, written by Robert Greenleaf. In it he wrote about our capacity to subordinate our own interests to the interests of others. The notion that the success of others should be more important than our own self interests. Greenleaf spoke about "wanting to serve others first to ensure other people's highest priorities are being served." He went on to say, "good leaders must first become good servants."

In many ways it's about learning to be humble. Even with as much emphasis as I put on service, I miss opportunities, or my pride or ego get in the way. Fortunately, my wife is happy to help me reframe my priorities and shape my perspectives in ways that are better and very helpful.

In 2000 I was serving as the global chair of the World Presidents Organization, a group of thousands of CEOs in scores of countries. Carson and I had been actively planning on taking approximately six hundred members and spouses to India for a week of learning in what was called a global university. The gathering in India was just terrific. The people, learning, and experiences were exceptional. All attendees were ready to return to their homes having gained much by their trip.

Prior to our departure we were able to have some business success, and I was feeling pretty good about myself. I suspect my wife sensed this in me, as she usually does. As I was preparing to return home, Carson informed me that we weren't going home, but rather we were going to Calcutta to work for Mother Theresa's charity. Specifically, we were going to work for several days at the Center for Dying Patients and several more days at the Center for Adoption of Special Needs Children. My wife always knows what's best.

We went to Calcutta, and it was an unbelievable experience. Carson had planned a remarkable opportunity for us in a true servant leadership way. During the first few days, we assisted those who were within minutes, hours, or days of dying. They spoke of their families, friends, and other special relationships. When you spend time with people who are in their last minutes, hours, days of life, you gain a different perspective.

The next week we were in a very large building with five thousand cribs of children ages one through five, all of whom had unique special needs—some were missing a leg, or an arm, or an eye, and some had other mental or physical disabilities. Most of these children would never be adopted. But all were needing love, attention, food, cuddling, and time.

They were crying, and they wanted attention. When we looked around, we quickly realized there weren't enough adults there to serve all the children. And so all we did, for a week, was hold babies, and love them, and hug them, and kiss them, and feed them.

The time we were able to spend with these special people left a profound impact on me. It helped change my perspective. It was a humbling experience, and I gained understanding. Those experiences allowed me to see more clearly how the human experience is so different for each of us and that I needed to be more focused on the needs of others. It was important for me to become more externally and other-centered and less internally and self-centered. It was an important and humbling reminder for me, thanks to my wife, Carson.

I have had the opportunity to travel the globe from a young age. I have been to almost every country in the world. I have seen abject poverty, great wealth, and everything in between. I am constantly reminded that people get along pretty well, but governments often times have difficulty with each other.

I am clear in my view that our communities and countries need our involvement at all levels. These very communities and countries in which we live are struggling as the world moves at an exponential pace. Many are being left behind as the gap between the haves and have nots grows ever wider. We must use our unique leadership skills and capacities to narrow the gap and fill in where institutions cannot. We must be bridge builders and communication facilitators.

Only people-to-people relationships have a chance to make the difference. Be that servant leader who sees the needs of others first.

We aren't better than. We are not less than. We are *equal to*, and we're all on this earth trying to do the best we can. Let's all lift where we stand.

Transactional versus Transformational Leadership: Brian Brault

I met Brian Brault about seven years ago, when he was a rising leader in EO. The people who knew him talked about his gentle leadership style and his capacity for being present and focusing on the individual with whom he was having a conversation or interaction. He also had the ability to stay centered on strategy, not tactics. He ultimately became the global chair of EO and led the board of directors on an interesting and strategic path, which was very good for the organization.

We have traveled the world together teaching the principles of leadership to young CEOs. In all of those travels, I have never seen him once stray from his personal values or deep faith. He has a strong intellect and a passion for helping others to see further down the road.

He had the good judgment to marry another outstanding leader, his wife, Jean. Together they are doing great work with couples and families by teaching practical ways in which marriages and families can be made stronger. I consider them both to be wonderful friends, and I have the highest respect and love for both. They have helped many to transform their lives.

One can live life by accident, or by design. Warren Rustand is one of the most purposeful people I know. His foundational principles for leadership have helped me to fully embrace living a life dedicated to a cause greater than myself. Many years ago,

Warren Rustand helped me to understand that my state of mind determines my future. Since then, I have no longer lived my life by accident. I live a life of meaning and integrity ... by design.

—Brian Brault, EO Global Chair 2017–2018,
Entrepreneur, Leader, Teacher

If you want to read what I consider to be the best book on leadership, read James MacGregor Burns's *Leadership*. Part of why it is so impactful to me is because it talks about the difference between transactional and transformational leadership.

Transactional leadership consists of the many things we do every day—our actions—that make us stand out, that make us a leader. *Transformational leadership* is to take that which lies unconscious in the human state and bring it to a conscious level. We can think of many extraordinary leaders who led by motivating, inspiring, and elevating others. Martin Luther King Jr., Mother Theresa, Winston Churchill, Mahatma Gandhi, Franklin Delano Roosevelt, and Nelson Mandela, to name a few. Each in their own way etched their place in history by transforming people, circumstances, and events. They were lifting where they stood.

When I had the opportunity in the nineties to meet with Nelson Mandela for a few minutes, I found him to be warm, gracious, and interested, and he asked good questions. I had studied his life from activist to Robyn's Island Prison to Pollsmoor Prison to president, and I had only one question to ask of him: How did he change and transform his life from prison to president?

He said he read the same poem each day, sometimes several times a day. Of course, I asked to which poem he was referring, and he responded, "'Invictus' by William Ernest Henley."

Perhaps by reading this you will understand him better, but you may also understand yourself better.

Out of the night that covers me, black as the pit from pole to pole,

I thank whatever gods may be for my unconquerable soul.

In the fell clutch of circumstance, I have not winced nor cried aloud,

Under the bludgeonings of chance my head is bloody, but unbowed.

Beyond this place of wrath and tears looms but the horror of the shade,

And yet the menace of the years finds, and shall find, me unafraid.

It matters not how strait the gate, how charged with punishments the scroll.

I am the master of my fate;

I am the captain of my soul.

Transformational leadership is the capacity to inspire and motivate others toward a higher place. By what we believe, what we do, and what we say, we are moved to look toward the greater good, the higher purpose, the nobler calling. We each have the ability to challenge people to look beyond themselves to find the deeper meaning, and in so doing we create a more meaningful life for ourselves.

RISE TO THE CHALLENGE

If you hear it, you will forget it.
If you read, you it will remember it.
But, if you do it you will understand it.

—Manchu Tribe

I believe the Manchu Tribe had it right. Only by doing the things that I have discussed in this book will one fully understand that about which I write. You see, this is our moment in history, this is our time to be who we want to be.

We must first do a course correction for ourselves so that we can lead others to do the same. We can change everything for our families, businesses, communities, and ourselves.

We have been given a gift, not only to understand these principles but also to apply them. We have the power to change our world, just as Brian, Eric, Kirsten, Jamie, Steve, Mary, Marc, Winnie, Reza, Natalia, Malik, and many others have done. Never underestimate your power to change your life.

My good friend, George Gan, from Kuala Lumpur, Malaysia, with whom I have traveled the world, speaking to entrepreneurial CEOs, talked with me about personal development. He said there are four stages of personal growth:

The first is dependence, which is when we are born and are nurtured by our families. They give us food, shelter, clothing, and the opportunity to grow.

The second is independence, which is when we leave home, make our own choices, and live independently.

The third is interdependence, which is when we learn that the world works best when we interact and work with others. It is our time of collaboration with people and the world.

The fourth is transcendence, which is when we understand that there is a higher calling and a greater purpose for our lives.

There is more than the acquisition of material things; there is the opportunity to help others. This is when we fully realize that we should live a life of contribution.

Conquering Mount Everest: Shailee Basnet

Shailee Basnet is a good example of the four stages of life. I met her in 2017 at a leadership conference in Katmandu, Nepal, where we had both been invited to speak and where I learned of her life story. She grew up in a middle-class family in Katmandu. She attended the university, majoring in business information systems (not journalism), and she spent the first few years of her professional life practicing journalism.

She was given the opportunity to participate in a mountaineering course to determine who could join a team to scale Mount Everest. At first glance, she is an unlikely candidate for the school or for climbing Mount Everest. She stands about five feet tall and must weigh only ninety pounds. Yet each time candidates for the expedition would get to a point of elimination, she was somehow always advancing to the next trial. (There was no process of elimination as such, but expedition candidates dropped out for various reasons.) In the end, she was one of the few who actually endured and proved qualified to climb the tallest mountain in the world.

She indeed climbed Everest and became one of the few women to do so. She believed that her team could reach new heights, so she led the Seven Summits Women Team, the first female group to scale the seven highest peaks on the seven continents.

She strongly felt that mountaineering had the power to empower other women. Therefore, following the expeditions, Shailee and her colleague trained young women survivors of human trafficking and showed them a better, more fulfilling life.

In her spare time, she is a stand-up comedian, often appearing at the Gotham Comedy Club in New York City. She brings joy and happiness to each of her interactions with others. She is a good friend in whom I find much to admire.

She rises to each challenge before her.

Warren is a true friend, champion, and mentor who cheers and supports you without making any uproar about it. What inspires me the most about him is his dedication to mentoring a generation of leaders to become not only better entrepreneurs but also caring family members, conscious citizens, and whole individuals. In reality he is passionate about creating a better world. I just want to know, where does he get all that energy from? He is a master at sharing an entire lifetime of experience in little nuggets of wisdom, be it in a quick, friendly piece of feedback or in an entire program on advanced leadership. He is a living Yoda that everybody needs in their lives!

—**Shailee Basnet, Coordinator, Seven Summits
Women Team (world's first female group to scale
the seven summits), Speaker, Stand-up Comic**

Four Things That Never Return

Omar Ibn Al-Halif wrote something a long time ago that resonates with me. I read this over fifty years ago, and it has been a part of my life since.

Four Things Once Spent Never Return in One's Lifetime.

The Sped Arrow

The Spoken Word

The Wasted Second

The Neglected Opportunity

The sped arrow is the act of violence. Once inflicted, it cannot be rescinded.

The spoken word are those things which are said which injure a person's heart.

The wasted second is our frivolous use of time, assuming we will always have more.

The neglected opportunity is our lack of learning readiness when opportunity knocks.

The principles we've discussed will benefit every aspect of one's life. They give purpose and direction to all the major areas of living: family, business, community, and self. We have the ability, capacity, and time to alter those things about our lives that we want to change. Let's live our lives in the most efficient, effective, and productive way possible.

First, let's seek clarity of vision in all things, large and small.

With that clarity, let's have certainty of intent as we act on our vision.

Then, let's use the power of our values to define our journey.

And lastly let's apply the Five Principles of Personal Greatness in what we do each day. This thoughtful application will allow us to move forward faster and with a greater degree of certainty than we have previously experienced. I am reminded of the quote: "If not me, then who? If not now, then when?"

> We have the ability, capacity, and time to alter those things about our lives that we want to change. Let's live our lives in the most efficient, effective, and productive way possible.

Live your life exactly as you intend. Live your purpose as you define it. We have just one chance to live our life in the way that is most satisfying to us. Why would we do otherwise?

We have been raised up to be exceptional. We have been raised up to be extraordinary. We have been raised up to be warriors. We have been raised up to be remarkable leaders in our homes, businesses, communities, and to ourselves.

Let's accept the challenge to be our best self. Let's raise our lives to the next level. Let's be our best when it matters most. Let's accept the higher calling.

ABOUT THE AUTHOR

Warren Rustand is a husband, father, grandfather, entrepreneur, corporate leader, educator, speaker, and philanthropist. He received his undergraduate and graduate degrees from the University of Arizona, where he was an Academic All-American basketball player.

In 1973 he was selected as a White House Fellow through a nationally competitive process. He was appointed as a special assistant to the secretary of commerce and in that capacity co-led the first-ever executive-level trade mission to the Soviet Union. He then became special assistant to then vice president Gerald Ford. In 1974, when the vice president became president, he asked Warren to serve as the appointments secretary and cabinet secretary to the president.

Following his time in public service, Warren again entered the private sector as an entrepreneur. He subsequently was CEO of six companies and chairman of many others. He has served on the boards of directors of some fifty-two for-profit and not-for-profit organizations. He was CEO of Providence Service Corp., a $2.1 billion company; Rural Metro, a $600 million company; and TLC Vision, a $400 million company.

For thirty years Warren led a public policy conference in Washington, DC, called "Public Policy and the Private Sector." Over those years some six thousand CEOs participated in the program, which included meetings with the president, vice president, cabinet secretaries, Congressional leadership, members of the Supreme Court, and leading lobbyists and journalists.

Warren was global chair of the World Presidents Organization and is the current dean of learning for the EO Global Leadership Academy, in addition to all Regional Leadership Academies. He is a well-known speaker on topics of leadership, personal development, strategy, scaling businesses, entrepreneurship, and family.

He has been recognized with many honors and awards, among them The Visionary Leadership Award, The Distinguished Citizens Award, The 25th Year Achievement Award, The Sports Hall of Fame, The Robbie Award, honorary lifetime membership in EO, chairman emeritus of multiple boards, and Father of the Year Award.

Trust and respect are central to effective leadership, and there is no more trustworthy advisor on the topic than Warren Rustand. He offers practical advice that is immediately actionable— advice that has transformed my leadership, my business, my relationships, and my purpose in making the world a better place.

—Marsha Ralls Hershman, CEO of The Phoenix Wellness Retreat, Author of *Rising from the Ashes*, EO Member

Warren brings a uniquely informed perspective to the topic of leadership, one that is highly principled and values-driven and grounded in a philosophy of respect for the individual and empowerment in terms of professional, personal, and spiritual growth. In his wealth of life experiences to date, he has demonstrated an unceasing ability to declutter the exercise of leadership in a way that applies seamlessly to groups of all sizes and orientation—familial, organizational, community, governmental, and so on—and resonates easily and logically on an entirely personal level. I have learned much from his guidance and good counsel over the years. You will too.

—Peter Reikes, Vice Chairman, Stifel,
   Nicolaus & Company, Incorporated

Of the amazing influences that I have been blessed with in my life, Warren Rustand has stood alone as the single greatest example of a man whose purpose for being is lived out at every moment with every breath he takes. Warren has coupled great intention with principles that he has honed over fifty years and utilizes them every day with the published purpose of "uplifting others wherever he can." My life has forever been altered in amazing and positive ways through his example and through our friendship. Warren's legacy will include this amazing book where he has unwrapped a large part of the secret da Vinci code of the key principles for leadership.

—Benjamin B. Richter, CEO, Bradford Logistics

I have been a friend and associate of Warren Rustand for thirty-five years. His sphere of influence, experience, and relationships is immense. During my time with him, I have seen him apply the principles and concepts he espouses every day in his personal and professional life. His personhood, constancy in purpose, and attitude toward everyone he knows continue to be a source of inspiration to me. I've spent many hours seeking and receiving advice from Warren on a wide range of issues and day-to-day challenges. I always come away from those conversations convinced I can be better and with work become anything I desire to be. He has always treated me as I can become, not as I was nor what I might be today. That propels me.

—Jay Stallings, CEO, Banner Washakie Medical Center

Warren Rustand, the man, his words, his philosophy of life and leadership, have changed my life in profound ways. I have never met anyone who lives his truth more than Warren does. In getting to know Warren and observing his style of servant leadership, I came to develop my own. As I learned at his side, I began to use his principles to develop myself. I learned that when I was a leader who led with clarity of vision, certainty of intent, and with the power of my values as my North Star, I would be most influential and would be in the best position to support and lift those around me. Warren's book, his words and principles, will change your life if you commit to them, live a life of purpose, and act with intent.

—Andrea Herrera, Founder, Amazing Edibles Catering and
    Boxperience and Global Leader, Entrepreneurs Organization

Warren Rustand has spent a lifetime guiding and mentoring men and women across the world. Having known him since college in the mid-1960s through athletics and business, I've greatly admired and respected his equanimity and compassion. This book is a testament to what he stands for and the precepts that will guide the reader to a cogent mindset on not only how to succeed in business but also how to better your life through proven principles that enrich one's character. Warren's codes of logical discipline and attitude are proven ways to benefit not only you, your family, and your profession but also ultimately humanity and the world. The values set forth here are true keys to lasting success and happiness, which come as gifts from Warren to you through his lifetime of experiences.

—Terry Dewald, Author, Former Professional
   Athlete, Art Dealer, Appraiser

In today's geopolitical and business ecosystems, leading with clarity of vision, certainty of intent, and a set of values are sorely missing traits. Many of us have encouraged Warren to document his principles of leadership because we have been blessed with his mentorship. Warren's foundational principles of leadership and application are living philosophies in Warren's life, not pop fictional or academic in nature. Honed by his many successful years in executive leadership, these principles have proven to be effective in many different situations and scenarios. His businesses followed them, his family believes them, and Warren lives them.

—Robert Samuelsen, CFO, Regional Transportation Authority

No man other than my own father has had a greater impact on my life than Warren Rustand. I have had the great pleasure of spending time with Warren and hearing him speak to these principles and values many times, but more importantly I have watched him live them with authenticity. For anyone committed to becoming a better version of themselves, this book is a must read.

—Steve Kearley, President, BENSON KEARLEY IFG

It is wonderful that you are memorializing the principles you constantly espouse in all that you do by writing a book. You have been a visionary to me. I've lived my life with principle and purpose, but hearing the concepts from you gave me clarity and enabled me to focus. Every conversation we have, or talk you give, causes me to focus and recommit to those principles. Your discussion this week about relevance helped me focus again. Thank you for sharing your wisdom and your friendship.

—Paul Robshaw, Chairman and CEO, AIC Ventures

Warren's teachings are a timely reminder of what leadership should be: calm, disciplined, thoughtful, and planned. After working with Warren, I crafted a family mission statement with my husband and our two teenage boys. The mission statement has been in place for ten years and has helped to guide decisions on universities, career paths, and our purpose as a lifelong team.

—Julie Walters, Founder of Raremark

I have known Warren for over thirty years. We served on the global board of directors for the World Presidents Organization, and I watched him lead as he served as the global chair of WPO. We also served on the board of TLC Vision, where Warren was chair, which is the world's largest LASIK eye surgery company. During our time serving together, I observed Warren practicing the very principles of leadership that he has written about in The Leader within Us. *These principles, when applied consistently, increase the opportunities for success for the individual and the organization. I have a personal testimony of the worth of these leadership principles, as I have applied them myself, and they have greatly assisted me in my successful leadership journey.*

—Toby Wilt, CEO and Entrepreneur

ACKNOWLEDGMENTS

To my friends from California High School and the University of Arizona, may I thank you for your good influence and modeling, which helped me grow and develop.

To my basketball teammates, who are very special friends and with whom I shared hard work, commitment, sacrifice, discipline, and success, thank you.

To my White House Fellow colleagues, each an exceptional person, thank you for your patience, friendship, and great example of public service and professional excellence.

To the friends with whom I worked in the White House, thank you for an extraordinary experience at such a young age, as it has shaped much of my thinking since.

To my fellow board members on the many not-for-profits where I have served, thank you for your example of servant leadership and caring for unique communities.

To my fellow board members of the for-profit entities with whom I served, thank you for your professional competence, guidance, and intelligence.

To my great friends in EO, YPO, and L3, your commitment to each other, learning together, experience sharing, and availability are legendary parts of our lives.

To my friends on the many management teams, professional colleagues, and partners, thank you for your example and the learning and fun we have had on our journey together.

My thanks to Alice Sullivan and Megan Rustand for their writing and editing skills, which have made this book much more readable.

CPSIA information can be obtained
at www.ICGtesting.com
Printed in the USA
BVHW020906261222
654950BV00013B/131/J